Elephant

Dan Wylie

REAKTION BOOKS

For Jill Wylie

Published by
REAKTION BOOKS LTD
33 Great Sutton Street
London EC1V 0DX, UK
www.reaktionbooks.co.uk

First published 2008
Copyright © Dan Wylie 2008

Printed and bound in China

British Library Cataloguing in Publication Data

Wylie, Dan
    Elephant. – (Animal)
    1. Elephants
    I. Title
    599.6'7

ISBN: 978 1 86189 397 0

Contents

1 Proboscidae

Let me begin in my own home, perched on the coastal escarpment of South Africa's Eastern Cape province. I have just spent some fifteen years researching and publishing on early Zulu history; not once in that time did anyone ever give me a Zulu-related memento or artefact. Within months of announcing that I was involved in researching *elephants*, however, I found my cottage inundated with 'elephantiana': T-shirts, calendars, mugs and cushion covers, postcards made from elephant-dung paper, a leather keyring from Singapore, a soapstone carving from Zimbabwe, a Ganesh statuette from Mumbai and a German-made Steiff limited-edition, collector's-item furry replica of baby Indian elephant 'Kandula', born in Washington, DC's National Zoo in 2001 and named Kandula – Sinhalese for 'strength' – after a Sri Lankan war-elephant. It shows how fondly fervent a lot of people are about elephants, as well as how commercialized elephant images have become, even as actual elephants worldwide have declined rapidly in numbers. Almost everyone I speak to has an elephant story or can tell me about another book, picture or *objet d'art*. Elephants populate the global consciousness more deeply and emotively than perhaps any other species, bar dogs and cats, so forgive me if this book misses your personal favourite one.

Named for a famous Ceylonese war elephant, 'Kandula' was born in the Washington Zoo, and is marketed as an individually numbered, cuddly collector's item.

A couple of centuries ago, the coastal plain I gaze across virtually swarmed with elephants. European ivory hunters and 'sportsmen' obliterated them. Now I'm just thankful that I can drive westwards for an hour to the Addo Elephant Park, where I can calmly observe, almost at arm's length, the 400-plus descendants of the only surviving elephants native to this province.

Not far from Addo, in the hills behind the industrial town of Uitenhage, a cave wall bears ochre paintings of elephants, executed by Bushman or San artists, probably several hundred years ago. Other Bushman art in southern Africa dates back an awesome 25,000 years, and doubtless in the million or so years before that evolving hominids lived alongside evolving elephants. As far as we can tell, both began in Africa.

And I don't have to go far from my cottage to find local crags whose crevices are alive with the dumpy, scurrying figures of the elephant's closest living relative, the rock hyrax or cony, locally known as the dassie. It seems quite a stretch of the imagination, but then 'closest' is deceptive: elephants and dassies hark back to an as yet undiscovered common ancestor that lived around 60 million years ago. So too, amazingly, do the manatees or sea cows. Elephants, for obvious reasons, were once grouped with the rhinoceros and the hippopotamus as 'pachyderms', the 'thick-skinned ones'. One major academic journal is still called *Pachyderm*, which publishes studies on rhinos and African (but not, oddly, Asian) elephants, even though the grouping has become taxonomic history. Rather, the links with hyraxes and manatees, implied by foot structure and dentition, are now being confirmed by DNA studies, as well as the ongoing discovery of transitional fossils on the North African coasts. There, in the shallows of the Mediterranean's geological precursor, the Tethys Sea, the manatees evolved into their present aquatic niche.

More recognizable elephantine ancestors – Proboscidae, or trunk-snouted mammals – also appear to have emerged first in North Africa. At least, that's where the oldest fossils have been found, around 40 million years old, in the sands of the Fayoum in Egypt, once a lush depression in the land. It's not clear, however, whether these somewhat hippo-like, probably amphibious and herbivorous creatures, the moeritheres, were true Proboscidae; the same uncertainties surround the contemporary barytheres, though these animals had the extended incisors that would evolve into elephants' tusks, and the beginnings of the 'conveyor belt' system of replaceable teeth.

The family Proboscidae, a name invented by German naturalist Carl Illiger in 1811 (*pro* = forward, *boskein* = mouth), really comes clearly into focus in the Miocene period (24 million years ago). Then, the deinotheres, 'terrible beast', after their fearsome four tusks, whose skulls show all the signs of having carried a genuine trunk, spread from central Africa both south and north as far as eastern Europe; they are not direct ancestors of the elephant, but lasted for an astonishing 20 million years. Over this period, doubtless due to climatic and vegetation changes, they changed, mainly in becoming bigger, some species reaching over 4 metres in height. *Deinotherium giganteum* would have dwarfed a modern elephant, and had powerful down-curving tusks, possibly used for digging. There were associated changes in dentition, too, grinding molars becoming more frequently characterized by ridges suitable for shearing

Elephant ancestors: a page from Raman Sukumar's *The Living Elephants,* drawn by J. Ramesh.

Moeritherium

Numidotherium

Deinotherium

Palaeomastodon

Gomphotherium

Platybelodon

(known as hypsodonty). Primarily, things during the Miocene dried out, forcing animals to adapt to expanding grassland conditions and tougher browsing, and land bridges opened up new opportunities for migration.

Other Miocene Proboscidae also originated in Africa, and eventually colonized every land mass apart from the islands of Greenland, Antarctica and Australia. Amongst them were the Stegodontidae, whose exact evolutionary relationship with the true elephants remains somewhat controversial. The best-known stegodon, *Stegodon ganesa*, evolved in Asia alongside the African elephantid lines, and so was named after the Hindu elephant-headed god Ganesh. Though not therefore in direct genetic line, *S. ganesa* displayed many characteristic elephantine features, including long and elegant tusks – possibly a case of convergent evolution. Recent fossils unearthed from sand pits in Thailand and China have complicated the picture: magnetostratigraphy, which dates sediment layers more precisely than ever before, indicates that some of these stegodontids predate the earliest African examples, so maybe some migrations went the other way. Moreover, still-tentatively classified subspecies of stegodontids migrated and differentiated throughout China and across the Japanese islands.[1]

There were also the ponderously named and pig-like gomphotheres (from *gomphos*, a 'bolt', hence stiff, and *theiron*, 'wild animal'). The gomphotheres are a rather loose grouping: elephant biologist Jeheskel Shoshani has called it a kind of 'wastebasket' into which anything that couldn't be fitted into a family line could be dumped.[2] Some species of gomphothere also grew larger over time, presumably to cope with having to eat greater amounts of less nutritious foods. Shoshani distinguishes two broad groups: the short-jawed and the long-jawed. The long-jawed, or 'shovel-tuskers', like *Platybelodon*, had bizarrely extended lower tusks formed like scoops, useful, one imagines, for digging up plants in shallow waters.

The short-jawed varieties included *Mammut americanum*, the mastodon. The fossil record improves in this case: many Pleistocene skeletons have been exhumed from American swamps, most famously La Brea tar pits, now surrounded by the city of Los Angeles. The mastodons carried tusks on both upper and lower jaws, the upper ones, extravagantly curved, sometimes reaching a massive 3 m in length and 25 cm in diameter. Their teeth were clearly distinct from those of the mammoths and other true elephants, having high rounded cusps (indeed, they are named for them: *mastos* meaning 'nipple').

At much the same time, other species of Proboscidae were radiating from Africa, especially during the Pliocene period. Amongst them seems to have been that intermediate form known as *Primelephas* – 'first elephant'. A wealth of fossils

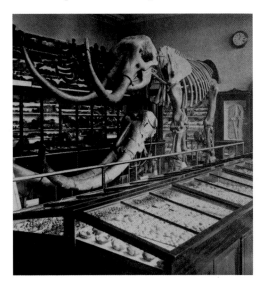

The mastodon skeleton formerly on display in the British Museum, London, photographed in the 1870s by Frederick York.

unearthed in sub-Saharan Africa, especially Kenya, indicates that this ancestor probably evolved from the gomphotheres rather than the Stegodontidae. It's hard to say, however, as there were so many types co-evolving. For a time, the 'splitters' amongst taxonomists prevailed over the 'lumpers'; in the 1930s the famous naturalist Henry Osborn distinguished over 350 species of proboscidae. Today, some sanity has prevailed, and a mere 163 different species, in 39 genera, now grace the proboscidean family tree. But as Jeheskel Shoshani notes, an element of subjectivity is always present in the interpretation of inevitably scant remains.[3]

The family Elephantidae was established by J. E. Gray in 1821. This family, evolving during the late Miocene period, was extraordinarily diverse, including some 22 of the 39 or so known genera. It includes the woolly mammoth, now most familiar to our youngsters from the charmingly grumpy character of Manny, aka The Heavy, in the *Ice Age* cartoon feature films, but also the subject of many novels ranging from J. H. Rosny's *Quest for Fire* (1911) to Jean M. Auel's *The Mammoth-Hunters* (1986). It has also been the subject of fascinated artists, from Neolithic cave painters to Rudolph F. Zallinger, whose mural *The Age of Mammals* in the Peabody Museum of Natural History at Yale in New Haven, Connecticut, is dominated by a mammoth. A film of *Quest for Fire* was made in 1981: a herd of elephants dressed up in shaggy coats to resemble mammoths are pacified by Neanderthals with handfuls of grass, whereupon they obligingly go off to stomp out the Neanderthals' enemies. As Eric Scigliano has said in his fine book *Love, War and Circuses*, the scene is 'supremely silly, but points up something plaintively real: humankind's abiding fascination with and affection for elephants'.[4] Even more massive than a modern African elephant at up to seven tons, and made still more imposing by its woolly coat and curling tusks, the mammoth has become a by-word for enormity: Mammoth Cave in Kentucky, to take just one example, has nothing to with the animals at all – it's just huge. (Not to mention the 'mammoth sale' at your local furniture store . . .)

The mammoths too originated in Africa, but have become most strongly associated with the northern hemisphere, where in both North America and Siberia complete bodies have been found frozen solid in the permafrost, their stomach contents intact and their flesh still edible. The most celebrated discovery was one of the earliest, in 1806, by a Scottish botanist, Michael Adams, on the River Lena. He was following up earlier reports that the local Tungu people had in 1799 found a mammoth body frozen into an ice wall, complete with skin and hair; they had avoided touching it, believing it cursed. Indeed, the nomadic peoples of both Siberia and China accorded the mammoths legendary status. The so-called 'pope' of descriptive

A cast of 'Dima', a baby mammoth exhumed from the Siberian ice; note the tufted ankles.

zoology, Alfred Edmund Brehm, recounted that some Chinese, by way of explaining heaps of gigantic bones, conceived that mammoths were giant underground rats which 'found sunlight hurtful' and 'perished as soon as [they] came into the open air'.[5] So reported a Dutch traveller named Nicolaas Witsen in 1692; Witsen is said to have coined the word mammoth, possibly based on Russian or Estonian words derived from *mamma*, earth, and *mutt*, rat.

Rock painting of a mammoth, usually labelled 'with enormous feet', but clearly a baby with heavily tufted ankles.

At any rate, greed got the better of the alleged curse in Adams's case; the Tungu chief sold the tusks for a pittance, perhaps the first recorded sale of mammoth ivory. (Much later, in 1989, when trade in elephant ivory was suppressed, mammoth ivory began to circulate more widely instead.) Adams was left with a mouldering heap of bones, skin and fur. Of the last, he gathered some 38 pounds, some strands of it 2 feet long – 'irrefutable proof that the mammoth lived in a cold climate', as Brehm wrote.[6] The skeleton now resides in the Mammoth Museum in Yakutsk where, as its website quaintly puts it, 'in bowels of Yakutia is found out a significant part of all unique finds of mammoths'.[7] Another famous carcass, named 'Dima', a baby found on the River Kolyma in Siberia, was so intact that even blood cells and individual proteins could be extracted for analysis. Some DNA has been sequenced from 28,000-year-old mammoth material by an American-Canadian team led by Stephen Schuster.[8] This has given rise to some probably premature speculation that mammoths might somehow be cloned or resurrected.

The excitement of such discoveries, and the clash of Western science with local cultures, has scarcely diminished. The nomadic Dolgan hunters of Siberia's Taimyr Peninsula, while happy to lead fossil hunters to mammoth remains, still regard them as huge mole-like rats with the potential to curse the communities that disturb them: in 1999, when the so-called Jarkov mammoth was airlifted out intact in a 23-ton block of ice, to be stored in an ice cave 322 km away, the Dolgan sacrificed a precious white reindeer to appease the spirits.[9] (The Americans, by contrast, made a film out of it, *Raising the Mammoth*, narrated by Jeff Bridges.) Not that the West had been immune to wild mythology: from the time of St Augustine on, mammoth bones were long used to support the pseudo-science of 'giantologie' – the 'study' of that mythical time when the earth was allegedly populated with giants.

But the most enticing question has always been: what caused the mammoths rather abruptly to die out? Brehm put it succinctly in 1860:

> Nobody could explain the sudden disappearance of the beasts of this region. Some, on the basis of vegetal remains, entertained the idea of a sudden change in the earth's axis of rotation; others tended toward the notion of a flood that might have submerged Siberia.[10]

A century later, Immanuel Velikovsky, in his infamous *Worlds in Collision* books, used the disappearance of the mammoth as evidence for an abrupt and catastrophic shift of the Earth's axis; and you can read the latest version of a well-read but unconvincing post-biblical Flood scenario by creationist Michael Oard on the 'Answers in Genesis' website (Oard carefully avoids dating anything, and fails to explain how mammoths – or elephants – might have fitted onto the Ark).[11]

Arguments continue. Changes in climate were almost certainly part of the story, though as we now know from our own period of global warming, climatic effects can be highly localized and apparently contradictory. Around 2 million years ago,

MUSEUM OF ANCIENT HISTORY—BERLIN.

A 1917 US war propaganda cartoon by W. A. Rogers optimistically relegated Hindenburg's military threat to the 'Museum of Ancient History, Berlin'.

a mini Ice Age set in, though punctuated by warmer interglacial spells. Ice smothered Scandinavia, Britain and Canada. Sea levels dropped; land bridges formed while other areas were cut off; vegetation altered and competition for food intensified, all stimulating 'a great geographical expansion of the elephantids and a high rate of speciation and phyletic evolution'. However, as Raman Sukumar adds, 'At the end, the curtains also came down swiftly on a bewildering array of proboscideans, from dwarf elephants not unlike the moeritheres in size to the towering mammoths.'[12]

It was not just that mammoths got overwhelmed by encroaching glaciers, as the *Ice Age* cartoons might suggest.

Some argue that it was actually a warm spell 13,000 years ago – an abrupt and frightening increase of some 6 degrees in only ten or twenty years – that put an end to the heavily furred giants. But we also have to explain the apparently simultaneous extinction of a large number of other mammals (up to 90 per cent in some regions), as well as the demise of proboscideans at different times on other continents, including South America and Africa. David Webb, Dale Guthrie, Richard Kiltie and others have proposed various scenarios based on rapid changes in vegetation availability in an era of more violent seasonality. Despite this, some mammoths seem to have survived for several thousand years more: remains on the Wrangel Islands of Arctic Siberia date back only 4,000 years.

This means, of course, that mammoths shared their environments with humans, as evidenced by a number of examples in Neolithic rock art in Europe – notably the beautiful example at Pech-Merle in France. It's highly likely, then, that human predation was, at least in some places, a factor in the mammoth's extinction. A French civil servant, Jacques Boucher de Perthes, found woolly mammoth bones lying alongside human artefacts in a River Somme valley site in the mid-nineteenth century. Stone arrow- and spear-heads with the long hafts of the Paleo-Indian or Clovis peoples are to be found with mammoth remains across North America, mostly dating to around 11,000 years ago; these are suddenly replaced in the archaeological record by the Folsom culture's smaller weapons, associated with the remains of smaller species, suggesting that this was the time that the mammoths had finally expired. In a number of places across the globe, the disappearance of various megafauna apparently coincides with the appearance of humans. Some scholars have used computer modelling to show that even a relatively small but expanding band of humans could have an effect on animal populations so devastating that biologist Paul Martin has called it the 'blitzkrieg' theory.

Ross McPhee and Preston Marx have proposed, rather, that mammoths might have succumbed to some 'hyperdisease' carried by humans – partly because, despite some unambiguous instances of mammoth hunting on Jersey in the Channel Islands and in Germany, there is actually little hard evidence that humans hunted them that much. They might just as often have scavenged off naturally dead carcasses, or taken out enough vulnerable calves to suppress breeding rates. As anthropologist Gary Haynes of the University of Nevada in Reno sums it up: 'A sweeping conclusion that would indisputably pin the blame for proboscidean extinction on Clovis hunters would be a literary triumph but a scientific impossibility.'[13] Most likely, human predation on this gigantic mobile source of food and artefacts was just the culminating factor in an already dire climatic situation.

At least in North America, the most recent theory proposes, the mammoths, along with other species that included Clovis humans, were wiped out by the effects of a comet strike or near-strike. The evidence lies in a thin layer of carbonated material – but none of the iridium associated with meteorites – discoverable over huge stretches of the continent, dating uniformly to around 13,000 years ago.[14]

The familiar woolly mammoth *Mammuthus primigenius* has become so strongly associated with the northern tundras (witness the charming poster compiled by the British Columbia Provincial Museum) that it's all but lost to sight that different species of mammoth appeared elsewhere, too. The steppe mammoth *M. trogontherii* lumbered across both the grasslands of Europe and the woodlands of England; the Columbian mammoth *M. columbi* was the largest of all and migrated as far south

OUR FIRST 100 YEARS

BRITISH COLUMBIA PROVINCIAL MUSEUM
100 MAMMOTHS – ONE FOR EACH YEAR – FROM THE IMAGINATION AND HANDS OF THE CHILDREN OF BRITISH COLUMBIA.

as Mexico. Even more interestingly, some mammoths and other elephantids that became isolated on various islands – Sumatra and Indonesia, Sicily and Malta – bucked the trend towards greater size and in time dwarfed down. The dwarf elephant *Elephas falconeri*, found on several Mediterranean islands, just reached waist height, as did the dwarf mammoths of the Santa Rosa islands off California.

In the proliferation of elephantid species between 2 and 1 million years ago, three genera would gain most prominence: *Mammuthus*, destined for early extinction; *Elephas*, to which the present-day Asian elephant belongs; and *Loxodonta*, the African elephant's line. All arose in Africa, migrating one after another, and sometimes alongside each other in direct competition. Adrian Lister opines that one European mammoth, *M. meridionalis*, might have been pushed into extinction by the appearance of the competing *E. antiquus*. Exact relationships between the three genera remain controversial: morphological characters suggest that *Mammuthus* and *Elephas* were closer to each other than either were to *Loxodonta*, though some genetic tracing suggests otherwise.[15]

The various species also evolved at differing rates. The rate is measured in Darwins, a unit invented by the great scientist J.B.S. Haldane in 1949 (1 Darwin = doubling or halving of a selected physiological feature in 1 My). The rates of change amongst elephantids has most accurately been traced through the hardest of all fossil remains, the molar teeth. Here, changes in number of plates, size and character of cusps and ridges, and densities of enamel, show that while *Loxodonta* evolved only at the rate of 0.1 Darwins, dwarfing could occur at a rate of up to 10 Darwins. The accuracy of our understanding here has been recently enhanced by advances in dental imaging, including a structure of dentin known as Schreger patterns, which are highly

Canada's British Columbia Provincial Museum commissioned children to draw their favourite mammoth.

Schreger patterns,
or 'engine-turning'
in a cross-section
of elephant tusk

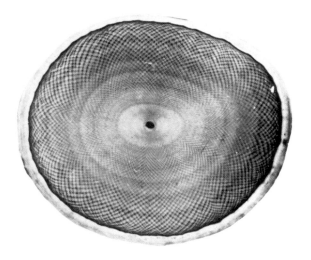

accurate in the discrimination of species.[16] Some tusks can in their tree-like layering yield a finely graded, even daily, impression of age and growth patterns, and can therefore cast a sidelight on changes in climatic conditions, food and habitat.

Some species could adapt quickly to environmental changes, but many could not. Those few that did – the three remaining species – probably survived because a mixture of specialized and generalized characteristics allowed them to adapt more readily. They too were the inheritors of long, diverse and entangled evolutionary lineages. The best-known species of *Elephas, E. recki*, excavated mainly in Kenya, gave rise to a number of other *Elephas* varieties, even as primitive forms of *Loxodonta* were evolving. One recent scholar believes the evidence shows that *E. recki* was not a single species at all, but more of a 'complex' of interrelated species.[17]

Why *Elephas* left Africa, and did not survive there, and why *Loxodonta* never left Africa, are unanswered questions. Quite how the modern Asian elephant evolved is also in doubt, because fossil remains are particularly scarce. Probably, the late Pliocene migration of one *E. ekorensis* split into different lines, including *E. planifrons*, a species well known from deposits in the Siwalik Hills of India. This was the direct ancestor of the modern Asian elephant, *E. maximus*. As for Africa, southern and central Africa were dominated by *L. atlanticus*, which died out as the *Elephas* species retreated, and the stage was left for our modern African elephant, *L. africana*. The two strains have never reunited. Though some Eurasian armies probably used both African and Asian elephants alongside each other, as we will see, there is only one recorded instance of a successful mating between captive African and Asian specimens: the tiny offspring died after only ten days. Union must remain a matter of imagination and advertising – as in huge billboards erected in Beijing for the 2006 China–Africa trade summit. Even Asian elephants have long since vanished from the whole of China, largely caused by human predation (which is why Mark Elkin

African elephants in China: a billboard in Beijing for the 2006 trade summit.

Indian elephant,
from Samuel
Daniell's
*Picturesque
Illustration of the
Scenery, Animals
and Nature
Inhabitants of the
Island of Ceylon*
(1808).

has titled his recent monumental environmental history of China *The Retreat of the Elephants*).

We are left with only a couple of taxonomic squabbles. While examination of both Asian and African haplotypes, based on mitochondrial DNA sequences, show that the two clades parted some 3 million years ago, DNA studies also track some of the differentiation within the two main species. Arguments have raged about whether or not a certain degree of differentiation justifies the declaration of separate sub-species or not. As Raman Sukumar writes, 'The molecular data from both Asian and African elephant populations, although still in early analysis, are already threatening to overturn the traditional systems of classification.'[18] The Sri Lankan elephants, though highly divergent in some respects, show a high degree of commonality of mitochondrial haplotypes with the mainland elephants, so there seems little support for a previous division into separate sub-species (*E. maximus maximus* and *E. m. indicus*). There is a certain degree of support for declaring the Sumatran and Malaysian elephants separate sub-species, but the jury is still out.

The African case is even more complex. In 1986 East African wildlife expert David Western investigated legends that there was a 'pygmy' elephant hidden in the forests of central Africa. Then in the 1990s a team led by Alfred Roca sequenced four nuclear genes from 195 elephants in 21 different populations, and concluded that there was sufficient justification for separating the savannah elephant (*L. africana*) from the somewhat smaller forest elephant (*L. cyclotis*). However, the picture is complicated by clear signs that the two had hybridized where savannah and forest abutted one another. Further studies have suggested that there are at least three, maybe five, fairly distinct populations, their differences probably accentuated by long separation, as humans have eliminated them from intervening areas and increasingly boxed them in. Interestingly, the forest elephants bear the most genetic resemblance to their Asian cousins. Sukumar opts for the safest response – that more work is needed – but acknowledges that these studies have 'opened up a virtual Pandora's Box of African elephant taxonomy'.[19]

We'll look more closely at present-day distributions in the final chapter. Let's return for the moment to something I mentioned early on: the fact that elephants and humans have virtually co-evolved in Africa. They have spread in waves across the world along similar paths – and if we believe anthropologist Gary Haynes, sometimes the exact same paths, humans padding along the dusty trails conveniently opened up by pachyderms. Ever since both species came into recognizable existence, they have probably killed one another in some places, and elsewhere coexisted peaceably or warily. This general pattern has not really changed. The perception that elephants and humans originated in the same space and time pervades many cultures, as we will see shortly. It's rather tawdrily summed up in a recent advertisement that evokes the savannah landscape in which both humans and elephants are supposed to have discovered themselves – grassland dotted with nutritious and sheltering trees. In this case, it's the marula tree (*Sclerocarrya birrea*), on which fermenting fruit elephants are exaggeratedly supposed to enjoy getting drunk – as are humans, by means of the marula liqueur being advertised. (I keep meeting people who claim to have witnessed this, but someone calculated it would take at least 200 kg of fermenting plum-sized marulas to turn an elephant tipsy.) The main line across the photo of elephants feeding on their arboreal sundowners reads: 'Our origins. Our inspiration.' *Hic!*

2 An Astounding Physiology

Anatomy, it might be said, is destiny.

The elephant's sheer size – 5.5 tons for the average African male – has made it irresistible to the mythographer, to the warlord wanting to terrify, to the hunter seeking his outsized trophy with his tiny copper-jacketed bullet, to the child at the circus, to the stroller in the zoo and to the modern game-park tourist. (Though he was probably wrong about the etymology, Isidore of Seville in the seventh century stated that the name *elefante* came from the Greek word for 'mountain', *lophos*.)

Massive weight means a massive intake of food, which dictates large feeding ranges, which in turn has produced perpetual territorial conflict with humans. The elephants' huge tusks, so beautifully textured for carving, has resulted in the deaths of millions of them. On the other hand, their awesome bulk and their stately shamble are awe-inspiring, giving off such an air of peaceableness and even sagacity that many of us can't bear the thought of them disappearing. Their often comical trunks and baggy hides are ripe for cartooning, too, and for charming small children with animal antics (scan the first 100 titles containing 'elephant' on Amazon.com: two-thirds will probably be children's books). The size and strangeness of our largest land-dwelling mammal are difficult to grasp: hence the famous parable (originally from Jaina teachings) about the blind men and the

A woodcut print by the Japanese artist Itcho Hanabusa (1652–1724), illustrating the parable of the blind monks and the elephant.

elephant. Each man, encountering so different a piece of the anatomy, deduces an utterly divergent picture of the beast to hand: rough and wrinkled; no, long and smooth; nonsense, it's snaky and hairy! As one stanza of John Godfrey Saxe's nineteenth-century poem, 'The Blind Men and the Elephant', put it:

> The First approached the Elephant,
> And happening to fall
> Against his broad and sturdy side,
> At once began to bawl:
> 'God bless me! but the Elephant
> Is very like a WALL!'

This story has entered world culture in the oddest ways: titles of articles from just one Internet database, for instance, include these: 'Language Awareness: The Whole Elephant'; 'Accounting and Operational Research: Trunk or Tail?'; and even 'Gene Expression Arrays in Juvenile Rheumatoid Arthritis:

The eroded surface of this elephant skull shows the honeycomb pattern of weight-saving diploe.

Will the Blind Men Finally See the Elephant?'. And Heathcote Williams, as the closing image of his poetic lament at the destruction of the elephant, *Sacred Elephant*, uses it again:

> In the story of the blind men,
> Each one gave a different description of the elephant,
> Depending on which part of it he felt.
> Now they are to be left
> Feeling only each other.[1]

Hopefully, it won't be quite that bad.

It takes a sturdy skeleton to support all that weight: a ribcage roomy enough for a golf-cart, a skull the size of an internal combustion engine. Yet the elephant moves surprisingly lightly. The skull is full of air cells called diploe, reducing weight. The huge leg bones are placed directly above one another, not at angles as in cats or dogs, but in an arrangement like a table, termed graviportal. This means that an elephant can sleep standing up, legs locked rigid. Some early writers thought they *had* to lean against a tree to sleep, with disastrous results if the tree fell over – a misconception, possibly resulting from a confusion with an equally imaginary elk (*alces*) described as early as Julius Caesar's *Gallic and Civil Wars* (Book 6.27) in the first century BC. In fact, those joints are remarkably flexible, like human knees, making them unexpectedly nimble climbers (good for circuses). All appearances to the contrary, elephants actually walk on tiptoe, as do most ungulates, with its foot bones all pointing down-

The number of toenails on an elephant's foot varies between front and back (usually 5 and 4) and between sub-species.

World-record tusks originally weighing 235 & 226 lbs shot on the slopes of Kilimanjaro in the 1890's

Probably the most massive tusks ever recorded, displayed here before a Zanzibar door, 1899.

Another enormously long set of tusks, hunted in the Sudan and photographed in 1923.

TUSKS OF A SOUDANESE ELEPHANT

A RECORD PAIR OF TUSKS PRESENTED TO THE NEW YORK ZOÖLOGICAL GARDEN BY THE LATE CHARLES T. BARNEY IN 1907. LENGTHS, 11 FEET 5½ INCHES AND 11 FEET. CIRCUMFERENCES: 18 INCHES AND 18½ INCHES. COMBINED WEIGHT 293 POUNDS.

wards and forwards and the load being taken on a pad of fat and connective tissue that spreads the weight evenly across the broad sole. A 9,000-lb (4,180-kg) Asian elephant was found to exert less than 9 lb per square inch (0.6 kg per square cm) of pressure underfoot – a feature that allows it to move easily through swampy or sandy ground, and with extraordinary quietness. Ranger colleagues of mine, camping in the open in Zimbabwe's Zambezi Valley one night, inadvertently laid out their groundsheet on an elephant path; in the morning they found an elephant's footprint square on the sheet between them, and they hadn't heard a thing.

The most prominent features of the skeleton are, of course, the tusks. These outrageously extended upper incisors have been both the elephant's main means of defence and its downfall.

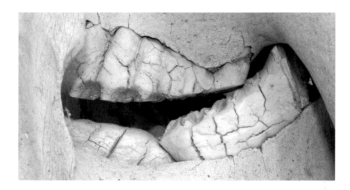

The conveyor-belt system of the lower molars; this elephant must have died well before its full life-span of 60-odd years.

Only two-thirds of the tusk shows outside the skin; under normal circumstances, it will grow continuously at a rate of about 15 centimetres a year. The biggest, mostly on African bulls, proved irresistible as trophies for European hunters. The largest recorded pair of tusks, from an African male elephant shot in 1899 by the slave of a Swahili merchant on the slopes of Mount Kilimanjaro (see page 31), measured over 11 feet (349 and 335 cm, to be exact) and actually now weigh around 435 pounds (198 kg); today they are in New York's American Museum of Natural History. Asian elephants' tusks are generally much lighter, though specimens of up to 9 feet (2.74 m) in length have been recorded. Carrying such heavy tusks has produced marked physiological compensations in bone and muscle structures in neck and skull. As far as the elephant is concerned, the tusks are excellent defence against its few predators, as well as being useful for digging for roots or water, stripping edible bark from trees, or lifting logs if the elephant is a captive worker. Sometimes the tusks are even used as a rest for a weary trunk.

For humans, the ivory of the tusk has been most attractive for its carvability. What makes it so different? A cross-section of a tusk shows a characteristic pattern of criss-crossing diamond shapes, known as 'engine-turning' – the evidence of tubules of dentine running through the tusk. The engine-turning pattern, unique to elephant teeth, is cross-hatched by concentric rings, rather like tree-growth rings, the result of both annual and seasonal growth phases. Untreated, dried-out ivory will crack along these rings. In fact, ivory is remarkably water-absorbent; some African peoples used tusks stuck in the ground as rain predictors. The composition of the ivory does appear to change markedly from one region to another: concentrations of calcium, phosphate, magnesium and other elements as well as amino acids vary significantly, leading Erich Raubenheimer, an expert on elephant dentition, to propose that such analyses could be used forensically to track the origins of poached ivory.[2] All in all, ivory is a uniquely pliable, yet resistant, material; no carver worthy of the name accepts a substitute.

The invisible teeth are as fascinating as the visible tusks. Unlike most mammals, which replace early or deciduous teeth with new ones growing up from below, elephants boast a mere six sets of brick-sized molars. These move forward, conveyor-belt fashion, as the front ones wear out and break; once the sixth set has been worn down, the elephant can no longer eat, and starves to death. So a fairly strict limit is set to an elephant's longevity: about 60 years, depending on diet and disease. Perhaps the fact that broken teeth might be found lying about with half-eaten branches or in elephants' faeces gave rise to the legend purveyed by Europeans in Renaissance times that elephants actively and secretively buried their teeth. However, the cunning Indians – according to one misguided commentator – were cleverer: they would plant bottles of water in places they thought teeth were buried, and those whose water disappeared, withdrawn by some 'magical power' by the teeth, would reveal their whereabouts. (Pliny, in his *Natural History*, fancifully

averred that the elephants knew the value of their own ivory, and would bury a tusk if it fell off.)

The surfaces of the molars are characterized by lozenge-shaped ridges, which are ground and scissored across the vegetation being chewed in a fore-and-aft motion; this lozenge shape, more diamond-like in the African than the Asian elephant, gave rise to the scientific name *Loxodonta*.

Of all skeletal features, one of the most fascinating is still poorly understood: the hyoid apparatus. This complex set of five bones provides attachment points for the tongue and for the larynx, and so is essential to eating, breathing and communicating. Moreover, it anchors at its base a pocket-like structure called the pharyngeal pouch, in which water is stored – a development thought by elephant biologist Jeheskel Shoshani to have evolved along with proboscideans' move into drier grasslands

Some argue that the elephant's trunk is evidence of aquatic origins; but it is also useful for playful wrestling.

Elephants are accomplished swimmers: some swim many kilometres between the Andaman Islands. Steve Bloom photographed this one in India in 2006.

around 25 million years ago. Uniquely amongst elephants, the upper and lower parts of the hyoid are loose and are probably implicated in the production of the elephants' rich range of infrasonic communication.

Other internal organs, many of them the subject of intensive recent study, also display unique features. The heart, for instance, weighing between 26 and 46 lb (12 to 21 kg), occupies a normal mammalian proportion of total body weight (about 0.5 per cent), but has a bifid or double-pointed apex instead of the usual single point. This is one feature that links it anatomically to sea cows – evidence, some argue, for elephants' aquatic origins. Some have suggested that certain features of the kidneys also point to that oceanic beginning, in particular ciliated ducts on the surface called nephrostomes; nephrostomes allow for osmotic exchanges with the blood and are found in sturgeons and frogs, but never in other viviparous animals. More prosaically, the kidneys, located high under the rear spine, are most important as a fat reserve, and the visible depression that develops there in an undernourished elephant is one indicator of health and environmental stress.

Of all the elephant's supposedly aquatic features, the respiratory system has invited the most controversy. It was observed early in the twentieth century that elephants have no pleural

Rudyard Kipling's own drawing for his 'Just-So Story' of 'How the Elephant got its Trunk'.

cavity for the lungs: the lungs are attached directly to the abdominal wall, and are pumped by muscular action. J. B. West, professor of physiology at San Diego University, has argued that this developed along with the trunk and a necessity for 'snorkelling' – swimming along with the trunk above water level. I've seen elephants doing this when crossing deep pools in the Zambezi Valley, but the evidence is as yet unconvincing that this activity was a primary evolutionary pressure for the elephant's peculiar respiratory system. The relative lack of scientific or fossil evidence for a gradual development of the trunk has even provided ammunition for some creationists to argue for God's more direct hand in the business. (Or one could simply offer Rudyard Kipling's famous 1902 'Just So Story', in which the original baby elephant finds his originally stubby nose caught in the jaws of a crocodile, and pulls, and pulls . . .)

At any rate, the trunk is a far more interesting and multifunctional instrument than just a snorkel, and surely evolved as the result of multiple stimuli. Hand, nose, trumpet, water-hose, weapon: the elephant's trunk is delicate enough to pick up a coin, powerful enough to smash a tiger to the ground. A combination of up to 100,000 longitudinal and radial muscles, with no bone or cartilage, makes it an instrument of extraordinary versatility. The Asian elephant's having only one 'finger' at its tip seems to render it no less flexible and sensitive than the African cousin's two-finger arrangement. Moreover, elephant anatomist D. Mariappan of Madras discovered that the elephant's trunk tip and the female's clitoris contained hypersensitive nerve bundles peculiar to the elephant. In honour of his mentor at the Institute of Anatomy at Madras, Mariappan named these 'Ayer's nerve endings'. Other studies show that many elephants appear to have left-trunk and right-trunk biases, rather like left- or right-handedness in humans, though the

evolutionary advantages or reasons for this remain obscure. The trunk is vital: an elephant without one, lost to injury or disease, quickly succumbs to starvation.

Other external organs are hardly less important. Perhaps least important to the elephant are the eyes, though to we visually orientated humans it's the eye that most often seems to connect us. The elephant's eye is somehow soft and imperturbable. Researcher Katy Payne recalls gazing into the 'patient amber eye' of an Asian matriarch: from that 'bulk flowing forward, huge and slow', the little eyes 'are looking down; the speckled ears are waving slowly and symmetrically in and out; the face – well, to call it a face'.[3] That an elephant does seem to have a *face* to which we can respond is graphically illustrated by the final photograph in Heathcote Williams's *Sacred Elephant* – a clever montage of two elephant eyes positioned to look, well, astonishingly human. On the other hand, you don't want to be on the

At least 20,000 individual muscles give the trunk its flexibility and strength.

receiving end of an elephant charge, with those same eyes fixed implacably on your destruction:

> Ndlulamithi raised his head sharply, as though to focus his amber eyes on us. We could not have been even vaguely discernible to him, as we were hovering well beyond the limits of his range of vision. His massive trunk coiled up menacingly under his chin. His ears were initially spread wide as he strained to listen, to pinpoint our position from any further giveaway sound that we might have made. Then those great ears were suddenly slapped tight against his head and he rushed towards us. I knew this was no mock charge; the silent message of deadly intent was unnerving.[4]

The huge ears (smaller in the Asian species) do more than signal aggression or calm. They are vital heat regulators, both through the network of veins close to the surface and through flapping cooling air across the shoulders. Researchers Polly

To look into an elephant's eye is to feel unquestionably considered, assessed.

An elephant's ears play a vital role in both cooling and communication.

Still from the film *Dumbo*.

The elephant's skin is a complete organ in itself, though lacking sweat pores.

Phillips and James Heath, using a combination of infrared thermography and a flat plate model, calculated that the whole of an elephant's heat-loss requirements were met by ear-flapping under normal conditions. (In a slightly bizarre extension of this research, Phillips and Heath also calculated heat-loss gradients in Walt Disney's cartoon elephant Dumbo, whose ears are proportionately a little larger than real elephants; they decided that the large ears were necessary to dissipate heat generated while flying at high speeds!).[5]

On the ears, the skin is less than 2 mm thick. Across the rest of the body, the grey, wrinkled, fissured skin is up to 2.5 cm thick, but it's still a sensitive organ. Almost hairless, except in the very young, and lacking sweat glands, the skin is vulnerable to irritation and parasites, mostly ticks, lice and warble-fly larvae, needing to be bathed in water and dust in a constant cycle. In the Asian elephant, pigmented patches often develop, especially around the face, resulting in a characteristic appearance of mottled pink. Exaggerated examples of this resulted in the mythology of the 'white elephant', still much sought after as symbolic of royalty. The kings of Siam were particularly famed for this desire; one such king, because elephants are pretty expensive to keep, used to make a present of a white elephant to courtiers he wished to ruin. Hence the term 'white elephant' for any grand fiasco involving spending more than you can ultimately afford.

Like any other complex organism, not surprisingly, elephants do suffer various diseases, mostly parasitic, both external and internal: flatworms, hookworms, roundworms and oestrid fly larvae in the guts of youngsters or in infected wounds. These are particularly prone to getting out of hand amongst captive elephants, or where overcrowded waterholes become infected through faeces. Raman Sukumar has published some admittedly tentative but intriguing studies of correlations between tusk size and parasite loads as retrieved from dung samples: the bigger the tusks, it seems, the fewer the parasites. Quite what this might imply is as yet unknown. Isolated cases of anthrax have also been recorded; at least one carver is supposed to have contracted anthrax from breathing in ivory dust. Infectious pneumonias, salmonellae and tuberculosis have occurred amongst captives. Dental infections can set in, particularly amongst the aged, as can arteriosclerosis, hastening the elephants' usually lingering deaths from malnutrition.

Asian mahouts, fondly bathing their elephants in the rivers of India and Burma, have understood these sensitivities, and much else, for at least 3,000 years. Good nutrition and skin care are obsessively tended. What might appear to us as rather comically unsightly bags of wrinkles are points of beauty to the

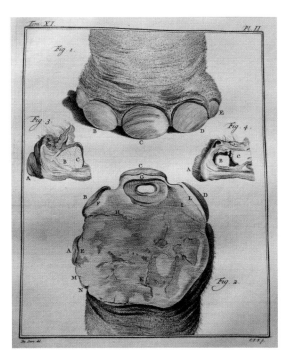

Pl. II

Fig. 1.

Fig. 3

Fig. 4.

Fig. 2

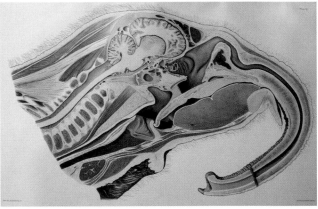

discerning mahout's eye: as J. H. Williams recounts in *Bandoola*, his lesser-known sequel to *Elephant Bill*, the loose flap of skin running from between the forelegs to the under-belly was known as the Pyia Swai, or honeycomb, and would be aesthetically judged. Indeed, there are sophisticated criteria for beauty amongst elephant handlers: proportions, head breadth and shape of bumps, tusk symmetry and thickness, length of trunk and overall height, all combine to produce subtly classifiable types of elephant elegance. Some, for example, are identified as *mriga* or 'deer-like' in physique, which is very different from *kumera* or 'royal'. Different regions can also be identified in their respective elephants' appearance: those from Kerala are said to be the most beautiful of all.

By contrast, in the post-Roman West, where elephants and their relatives had long been eradicated and only the rare excitement of a captive animal provided knowledge, all sorts of myths about elephant physiology abounded. It was only in the twentieth century that a sense emerged of how the elephants' physiology interacted with their ecology, and indeed with an intricate elephantine society. After the genocidal depredations of European hunters in Africa and Asia alike – hunters who saw elephants as no more than animated repositories of coveted ivory – the notion that elephants could possess a society at all came as something of a surprise. Today, elephant interactions are so intimately studied and known that not a few observers believe that *we* can learn something from *them*: 'The wisdom of the tuskèd domination/ Holds up to shame the apery of mankind', as a poem by Henry Harmon Chamberlin put it.[6]

So how does elephant physiology dictate behaviour? Two physical functions govern all: consumption and reproduction. Elephants are huge; they have to eat a lot. A 5-ton elephant will consume up to 300 kg – 6 to 8 per cent of its body weight – of

A study of the foot and a cross-section of the head of an elephant, illustrations from the Comte de Buffon's enormous *Histoire naturelle* (1749–67).

vegetable matter every day, which takes over twelve hours of steady feeding. Elephants will eat a wide variety of plants – hundreds of different species if available – ranging from tree bark to grass, gorging on fruits like tamarinds in Asia or marulas in Africa when they are in season. They will also seek out mineral supplements in salt licks or caves, and even create caves of their own; the most famous are the Kitum caves on Mount Elgon in western Kenya, enormous caverns largely created by elephants tusking out deposits of sodium-rich earth to supplement the inadequately nutritious forest diet of the area.

The digestive system, taking some fourteen hours to pass food through a 35-metre tract, is quite quick and provides sufficient energy, but metabolically it is rather inefficient: the process converts only about 22 per cent of the intake's protein. What eventually gets defecated – up to 100 kg a day – is a treasure-trove for dozens of other creatures, ranging from baby elephants ingesting crucial micro-organisms from the pre-digested adult faeces, through baboons to dung-beetles. (Amusing but serious signposts on the roads through Addo National Park in South Africa give right of way to dung beetles: they are that vital to the whole ecosystem.) Some species of plant, like certain acacias and (the most thoroughly researched) *Balanites wilsonia*, best germinate once they have passed through the acids of an elephant's gut, and the elephants are instrumental in dispersing them. There are a number of studies out now trying to determine the impact of hunting elephants on the germination patterns of such forest species.

Really dedicated elephant observers can even identify individuals by their dung. J. H. Williams, in *Bandoola*, describes the capacity of one forest manager in Burma to recognize each of 400 individual elephants' droppings, which he would carefully examine, 'prodding it with his shooting stick. Usually he had no comment to make, but occasionally he would say, "Look at that. Mee Too's been eating earth again. I don't like that." Prod, prod. "Um. Elephant-worms again." Or, "Poor old Kah Gyis. Beginning to show his age. Bamboos passing through him like tough string".[7] Ecology apart, elephant dung is pretty clean and inoffensive, and you can now buy all manner of greeting cards, envelopes and notepads made from rough-textured but attractive elephant-dung paper! A more controversial use of elephant dung involved one dab of it strategically placed over the nude breast of artist Chris Odili's 2004 multi-media work, 'Black Madonna', which offended New York mayor Rudi Giuliani so deeply that he threatened to close down the whole gallery.

It is little wonder, given the volumes of consumption involved, that elephants can be regarded as positively destructive of the vegetation around them, especially when confined to fenced-in areas much smaller than the vast ranges of yesteryear, and when artificial waterholes encourage elephants to congregate in more limited ranges. Given the freedom to do so, elephants will range over enormous areas. Walter Leuthold's studies of radio-collared elephants in Tsavo, Kenya, showed elephants wandering across an area of over 3,000 square kilometres, with distinct seasonal rhythms and preferences. The range will vary hugely, however, with differences in vegetation cover and availability of water. Though elephants have been known to survive without water for more than a week, under normal circumstances they will drink up to 200 litres a day. They will go a long way for it, and evidently have an excellent memory even for those spots in dry riverbeds where they have to dig deep holes to reach it. There are, however, few such free-range movements available to elephants nowadays.

Perhaps it is this necessity to remember far-flung spots that has helped develop a brain formidable enough also to hold a good deal of 'cultural' information. That 6-kg organ has been the subject of some intensive study. Though the elephant's brain is four times the size of a human brain, it occupies a much smaller proportion of total body weight. It nevertheless has a highly convoluted cerebrum and cerebellum, correlated with excellent cognitive and motor coordination. Rather than risk anthropomorphism by speculating about 'intelligence', some scientists now measure the 'encephalisation quotient' (EQ) – the relationship between actual brain/body-weight ratio against the expected ratio. In this scheme, humans have an EQ of 6, chimpanzees 2.5 and elephants 1.9. Your humble house dog has an EQ of 1, which is to say 'average'. A study of six Asian and six African elephants indicated a higher EQ value for the Asian, but it's too small a sample to conclude much from. The EQ is perhaps less important, however, than noting in the elephant the

The revengeful and chivalrous Elephant of Africa.

A true Story.

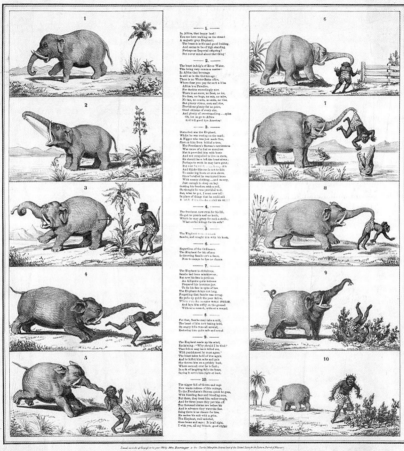

Composed, drawn and edited by John Boeringer, St. Louis Mo., Broadway 337.

For Sale at { Matt. R. Cullen, 63 North Fifth Street
Harris & Brent, 47 North Third Street } St. Louis Mo.

presence of an unusually large temporal lobe, which in humans has been shown to be particularly associated with memory. So there is at least some neurological evidence to support the legends of the elephant's monumental memory.

Others prefer to measure intelligence by observing behaviour. Over the last 30 or 40 years of study, particularly by a set of extraordinary women watching wild elephants in Africa for years on end, it has become clear just how complex and nuanced undisturbed elephant relationships are. Cynthia Moss is one of those women: for over 30 years she has lived amongst and observed the elephants of Amboseli National Park in Kenya. She has mapped the intricacies of family relationships, geographical movements and individual characteristics amongst hundreds of animals, recounting her discoveries in a remarkable book, *Elephant Memories.*

Perhaps at the forefront of such recent discoveries is the caring complexity of elephant family ties. Moss outlines concentric circles of relationship: a mother and her calf at the centre, enclosed in a wider circle of cows closely related to the mother, usually including an older matriarch, and their own juveniles. Outside that, a looser coterie of younger bulls hovers, gradually asserting their independence; and finally there is on the outside a scattering of bulls who spend much of their time alone, except for brief periods of mating activity. The central group may split and drift apart from time to time, but contact is always maintained, and reunions are tumultuous and joyous, as Cynthia Moss describes:

> The two subgroups of the family will run together, rumbling, trumpeting, and screaming, raise their heads, click their tusks together, entwine their trunks, flap their ears, spin around and back into each other, urinate and

defecate, and generally show great excitement. A greeting such as this will sometimes last as long as ten minutes.[8]

The core groups are devoted primarily to the raising of calves. A calf is 22 months in gestation (a span that, combined with sophisticated scanning and camera techniques, made possible an astonishing 2006 BBC film of a calf's development *in utero*). The youngster will remain with the mother for the first few years of its life. Both mother and 'aunts', or allomothers, rush to its assistance should it fall into trouble. A calf without allomothers is three times less likely to survive than one with four or more.

The essentially matriarchal structure of these elephant families has been seized on by some feminists as worthy of emulation. Whatever one thinks of that, the maternal care demonstrated by elephants can reach the marvellous. Veteran elephant researcher Anthony Hall-Martin related this incident amongst the aggressive elephants of Addo National Park in its early days:

I spent time habituating the elephants to me and my vehicle. When I began they would charge on sight, but within six months they were coming up and touching me. One day I was near the herd, with my wife Catharina and our new baby, Vega. I presented my first-born to the old matriarch, who I had got to know quite well. She disappeared into the bush and, a few moments later, reappeared with her new baby. She had come to show me her youngster. Now I am a scientist and have thought about that incident and I can't explain it – it was a moment of magic. There was a special bond between us for that moment.[9]

There is a long, sometimes exaggerated history of enmity between elephants and rhinos: an English magazine depiction of a rhino 'attacked by elephants', *c.* 1836.

Raising a calf is itself an intricate business – discipline, play, learning and safety all held in delicate balance. Education into elephant ways continues well into an elephant's 'teens'. In one recent, illuminating case, ten young bulls were translocated from Kruger National Park in South Africa to the Pilanesberg reserve. A bit like the boys in *Lord of the Flies*, the youngsters ran positively amok, to the extent of trying to mount and then actually killing several rhinoceros – wholly aberrant behaviour for elephants. However, the introduction of six older elephants rapidly calmed them and sorted them out, partly by suppressing the youngsters' too-early onset of musth, the state when testosterone rises.

(There are, incidentally, a number of testimonies to elephant–rhino relations through history in both Asia and Africa. Both the Romans and the Indian Mughals enjoyed pitting them against each other in the arena; the emperor Babur in sixteenth-century India hunted rhinos from elephant-back. One

52

nineteenth-century hunter in tropical Africa misguidedly claimed that they were sworn enemies. There are records of mutual aggression, and you can view an elephant–rhino 'face-off' on YouTube. More strangely, when in late 2007 three rhinos were killed by poachers in Imire private game reserve in central Zimbabwe, the orphaned rhino youngsters apparently found the domesticated elephants on the reserve something of a substitute.)

I observed another extraordinary example of elephant sociability at Imire. Owner Norman Travers, having obtained several orphaned elephants at different times, discovered that one old matriarch just didn't get on with the others and had to be enclosed in a separate area. There, lacking elephant company, she instead adopted a herd of buffalo. I watched them all following her in a long train towards water one evening, a couple of the smaller buffalo nestled up under her flanks. Even more remarkably, it transpired that when a buffalo calf was born, the elephant tended to kill it; possibly she didn't quite recognize them as buffaloes yet. The buffalo mothers – even those who hadn't experienced a personal loss – learned to go away and give birth in remote reed-beds, and only tentatively introduced them after a week or two, at which stage the matriarch seemed happy to accept them.

Further complexities are evident in sexual activities. Elephant cows come into oestrus at variable intervals, generally around every sixteen weeks. Hence, perhaps, elaborate rituals and signalling systems have developed. Bull elephants periodically enter that state known as musth, when testosterone levels rise and aggressive behaviour manifests: it is well known now that Asian mahouts who get killed by their own elephants are almost always attacked by an animal in musth. (Though not always: for one, 'Nellie' was a female Asian elephant held at

Asian 'composite' elephant, depicting Kama, the god of love.

Durban's botanical gardens who eventually killed her keeper.) Musth is visible in the leaking of dark fluid from temporal glands just behind the eye. This is the source of the notion that elephants cry; in fact – despite the title of Jeffrey Masson's famous book on animal emotions, *When Elephants Weep* – they have no tear ducts. Wafting its powerful scent ahead with its ears, a musth bull will approach a group of females, seeking out any in oestrus. He will explore the cows' genitals and temporal glands with his trunk, placing its tip against the specialized 'Jacobson's organ' located in the roof of his own mouth in order to assay their chemical readiness, a test known as flehmen. Much excited foreplay might ensue, with the female urinating and defecating, spinning around and finally running off, the bull in pursuit, dragging his distended penis, dribbling and green-tinged. (Cynthia Moss and Joyce Poole amusingly relate how worried they were at first on observing this 'green penis disease', as they initially termed it, thinking some dreadful communicable ailment was afoot.)

Given the enormity of the elephant member, it's surprising that it hasn't been more sought after by humans, like tiger penis or rhino horn. However, several cultures in both Africa and Asia have associated the elephant with sexuality and the passions. Classical writers like Pliny and Aelian alluded to elephants as lustful, but these passages were excised by later Christians, like St Francis de Sales, in the early 1600s, when the elephant became iconic rather of honesty and reliability, even chastity and good table manners![10] In India, Ganesh and his associated myths often emphasize a generalized fertility. A sub-genre of Indian painting, in which the shape of an elephant is constructed from human figures, usually women, is sometimes extended to a tangle of semi-dressed couples in variously graphic Tantric positions. According to that ancient sex manual, the *Kama*

The position of the breasts between the forelegs is another factor making elephants seem quasi-human.

Sutra, an elephant-woman or Hastini is the lustiest of women, crude and vulgar in her carriage. In Kerala temples, the most prized elephant was a bull elephant whose trunk, tusks and penis touched the ground; it was seen as representing absolute virility and was reserved for the shrine's chief deity. Modern 'magic' practitioners tout elephants as combining both responsibility and sexuality: buy a gemstone carving and 'If you want to be very sexual, rub Elephant with musk oil and place him facing your bed, this works for both sexes.'[11]

The odd fact that the cow's vulva faces forward led some early and uninformed speculators to depict elephants copulating face to face like humans. Their confusion was compounded by the position of the bull's testes within the body, not outside like other mammals', and the position of the cow's two breasts below the shoulders, also more like humans than dogs or antelope. However, the bull mounts quite conventionally from the rear, effecting brief entry with the aid of a sinuous s-bend to the penis. Having mated, the bull plays little further part in the core matriarchal group's activities.

An elaborate family and herd life goes along with a complex communication system, judged by many to be another crucial indicator of intelligence. If not precisely a language, elephant communication has nevertheless been recognized as extraordinarily intricate, and possibly dialectal. They evidently communicate a great deal through scent and chemical signals, especially pheromones, and perhaps even more through touch. Body language – ear movements, head position, trunk position, modes of walking such as the bull's 'musth walk' or the peculiar wary restlessness of an oestrous female – also conveys information at every meeting.

They also listen to each other. George McKay, working with Asian elephants, learned to distinguish a range of snorts, growls, rumbles, squeaks and chirps to which he could assign rough 'meanings'. Beyond the obvious elephant trumpeting, deep belly rumbles also communicate. And beneath that again, infrasonic communication happens, below the range of human hearing. McKay began to discern 'an almost inaudible purring' from elephants' throats. Katy Payne, standing next to an elephant in Washington Park Zoo in Portland, Oregon, one morning, became aware of 'a palpable throbbing in the air like distant thunder'.

Payne, modifying technology developed for the detection and recording of whale song, began to record this infrasonic realm amongst elephants in eastern and southern Africa. A whole world opened up: it became clear that elephants, rumbling to each other at frequencies between 14 and 35 hz, and up to 115 decibels, could communicate over hundreds of metres, possibly even kilometres. This explained observations by people overseeing elephant culls, like Rowan Martin and Garth

'Elephant grave-
yards' may be
a myth, but
elephants are
not immortal.

Thompson in Zimbabwe, that groups quite far removed from the scene of killing, certainly out of normal earshot, would simultaneously become agitated. Payne was able to distinguish at least eight different kinds of call and relate these to specific behavioural responses. (Payne titled the book she wrote on her research *Silent Thunder*.) Karen McComb, working with Cynthia Moss in Amboseli, worked out through carefully calculated playback experiments that a great deal of individual recognition was being relayed as well: a single elephant was evidently familiar with the individual calls of fourteen family groups, over 100 adult females in all. In one touching instance, playing back the call of a female already three months dead elicited a positive response from her closest relatives.[12]

This evident sensitivity to, and awareness of, the death of relatives is another aspect that invites close comparison to human intelligence. For thousands of years, bizarre legends of 'elephant graveyards' circulated. They are myth, though the tendency of dying elephants to drift towards areas with water or softer vegetation means that more might die in some specific areas. The legend continues to stimulate writers – though nowadays more likely in satirical vein, as in this stanza from a poem by South African poet Chris Mann:

> Those old hunter-types are gone,
> yet still the legend lingers,
> for elephants
> are ponderous, likeable, anachronistic beasts,
> and where better than Africa
> can old idealists go
> to lay their creaking structures down?[13]

Elephants' unusual awareness of death, and something akin to mourning, is nevertheless now well documented – probably,

A 19th-century British traveller, shown here in Burma sketching an elephant, reported being repeatedly deterred by the elephant throwing things at him.

58

Cynthia Moss writes, 'the strangest thing about them'. Many have observed how elephants try to revive dying siblings, mothers or offspring, and remain with the corpse for long periods, or return to it frequently. They sometimes throw dirt or branches onto a body, as if in a rudimentary gesture of burial. They often revisit the bones of a long-deceased relative, throwing them around, stirring them with a foot or exploring the crevices of the skull with their trunks. This is such predictable behaviour that filmmakers can lure elephants into choice positions by moving elephant bones there.

Yet another indicator of relatively high intelligence is a primitive form of tool-using, such as scratching inaccessible spots with a broken-off branch. Wild elephants observed in Nagarahole National Park in India routinely used branches to swat away irritating flies. Thirteen captive elephants, also at Nagarahole, were provided with a variety of branches as an experiment; eight of them quickly modified the branches by pulling unwanted bits off in order to fashion more effective fly-switches. Elephants' capacity to manipulate objects, of course, has been crucial to their use in circuses; some are still taught to throw darts at balloons and other silly tricks. One zoo elephant was, worryingly, hurling objects repeatedly into the rafters of her night-house; it was discovered that she was throwing them at scurrying rats, whether in irritation or amusement it would be hard to say. Elephants do often appear to have a sense of humour and mischief, as calves ambush one another or sling things at each other in fits of pique. Their capacity for altruism seems also highly developed: not only do they routinely help one another out of muddy fixes or crowd round to help an ailing member of the herd, but they have also been known to warn people of the presence of lions or puff-adders. This can go awry: there is a well-known story about an elephant who, having attacked an intrusive cattle-herder and broken his leg, then refused to let anyone else get near him.

This should not, of course, obscure less savoury aspects of elephant behaviour: bullying, occasional indifference to suffering, sometimes fatal aggression between competing bulls, a propensity to kill humans and destroy their crops and livelihoods. Nevertheless, almost all who have the opportunity to live amongst and alongside elephants in a non-threatening situation develop a powerful, sometimes mutual affection. Iain Douglas-Hamilton, a pioneer researcher, wrote in his ground-breaking book, *Among the Elephants*, that 'with other wild animals, elephants fulfil part of man's deep need for the refreshment of his spirit.'[14]

All in all, elephants display societal structures and behaviour so obviously complex, and so apparently close to the human, that more than one writer has wondered what it might be like to *be* an elephant. Do elephants have a remembered history? Do they have a sense of culture, even some self-awareness? What *do* they communicate to each other? Cynthia Moss inserts passages of near-fiction in her book, *Elephant Memories*, but doesn't try the impossible task of getting inside an elephant's mind. A Canadian novelist, Barbara Gowdy, does. In *The White Bone*, set in East Africa, Gowdy clearly draws on Moss's, Joyce Poole's and Katy Payne's researches to recreate elephant family life, historical memory and cultural awareness from the elephant's point of view. Gowdy portrays one elephant character attaining that iconic measure of self-awareness: recognizing herself in the fallen wing-mirror of a human's vehicle. (A 2006 scientific article in fact reported some clever experiments indicating quite clear self-recognition in mirrors by captive elephants.[15])

Whatever the possibilities, the view that elephants are so close to humans that they deserve special protection and attention has come to dictate many people's attitudes, and to affect management and even culling techniques. Dr Daphne Sheldrick DBE, who for five decades has studied Kenyan elephants from her base at the Nairobi Animal Orphanage, has no doubt that they are a 'kindred species'. Having hand-reared 75 orphans, she wrote in 2006, she 'can categorically state that they are, indeed, very human in terms of intelligence, emotion and a few additional attributes besides'.[16]

On the other side stand those scientists who regard the attribution of emotional states to animals as illegitimate anthropomorphism, and the presence of emotion either in the animals or in the human observer as clouding the real issues. 'Elephants are elephants,' as one anatomist has put it, 'not big, grey humans.'[17]

As we will see in the final chapter, where we review current conservation issues and look into the elephants' future, this debate is now hot. For now, however, let us turn to the astonishingly rich 'life of elephants' in the human imagination; their mythology, literature and art.

3 Representing Elephants

The world is awash with images of elephants. For every living, lumbering pachyderm there must be at least one poem, story, novel, coffee-table tome or television documentary; a hundred statues; a thousand paintings; tens of thousands of tourist trinkets; millions of postcards and advertising logos. Just about anyone you speak to has their favourite anecdote, book or photograph. This is the case even in places where elephants have never lived, such as North America. Some years ago I flew into Whitehorse, Yukon, about as far from southern Africa as it is possible for me to get – and there in the first coffee shop I entered was a wall covered in the proprietor's own photographs of Namibian elephants. Elephant collectibles are a serious industry: Michael Knapik, a collector who has produced his own encyclopaedia of elephant collectibles, found 3,000 elephant artefacts for sale on eBay in a single week, from dramatic realistic bronzes to cute plastic toys. I would hazard a guess that – maybe dogs, cats and horses excepted – no other single mammal has been so prominent in artistic representations of the animal world. It would be difficult to do full justice to this richness in a lifetime, let alone here.

This chapter starts, then, with the earliest rock art; then moves on to the earliest myths of origins and folklore; through the realms of religious iconography; the development of sculptures and paintings of elephants up to the present; elephants in their sundry literary appearances (in proverbs, hunters' memoirs, novels, poems, and as ubiquitous metaphor); and ends with the elephant in contemporary popular culture, from music and advertising to what is, no doubt, the medium of our time, film.

People have been depicting elephants ever since they could depict anything, it seems. Mammoths and elephants appear in many of the 75,000-odd known rock art sites across the world. There are several well-known cave paintings of the mammoth in Europe – at Font-de-Gaume, in France's Dordogne (*c.* 15,000 years old); at Vallon Pont d'Arc (17,000 years old), at Rouffignac (a small herd depicted) and most beautifully at Chauvet. In 2007 the subtle remains of a mammoth petroglyph were spotted in Cheddar Caves in Somerset, England.

Africa is even better endowed with rock painting and engraving. Some of the earliest is work from southern Africa by San or Bushman artists (just what to call this panoply of related but scattered peoples, speaking a multitude of mutually unintelligible languages, remains controversial). Wherever suitable surfaces in sheltered caves and overhangs presented themselves, Bushman

Raised trunks scenting the air; a San rock painting at Roussow, South Africa.

artists, for both shamanistic and, I would imagine, more prosaic reasons (like fun!), painted their local animals. At least some Bushman rock art is thousands of years old, ranging from a tiny 25 mm to the life-size paintings in Ruchera Cave in Zimbabwe's Mtoko district (dated to the ninth millennium BC). The depictions generally show elephants side-on, but there is also one depicting an elephant from behind, and one previously unpublished example, from the Roussouw district of South Africa's Eastern Cape, viewed head-on, trunk inquisitively raised. The paintings vary in colour from reds to greys, perhaps reflecting the colour of the local mud or dust the elephants would have basked in. Less colourful, but equally well observed, are rock engravings, mostly in Namibia. There, the shapes of the elephants seem eminently suited to the blue-black basalt boulders they appear on. Some scenes depict hunting, mostly with arrows but occasionally with hamstringing machetes. A few surviving Bushman communities remained elephant-hunting specialists until overtaken by European firearm technologies in the early nineteenth century. However, elephants were not merely food sources. Bushmen, unsurprisingly, incorporated the biggest animals of their experience into their spiritual belief-system, and one painting, from South Africa's Porterville area shows a herd enclosed within a double rainbow, presumably associating the elephants with religiously significant rain-creation ritual. At one time, most Bushmen believed animals *were* people, and this close ancestral relationship was captured in their folk tales as well. What may count as the earliest poem we possess about the elephant (depending on how many generations handed it down, and who can tell?) is a delightful Bushman couplet:

Tall-topped acacia, you, full of branches,
Ebony-tree with the big spreading leaves.[1]

Distantly related peoples, the pygmies of the Congo and Gabon, also mingled reverence and predation, as shown in one Beku pigmy song:

Through the forest whipped by rain
Father elephant treads heavily, *baou, baou, baou*
Diffident, fearless, proud of his strength
Father elephant, whom nothing can subdue
In the forest he shatters at will.
He stops, starts up again, browses, trumpets
Knocks down a tree or two, searches for his woman.
Father elephant, a distant hunter hears you.
Elephant hunter, take up your bow![2]

Less rock art appears in East, Central and West Africa (though there is a beautiful elephant outline at Kakapel cave, western Kenya). But North Africa, from Nubia to Morocco, is replete with elephant depictions. Though they are difficult to date precisely, some are thousands of years old. The particularly finely executed examples from Chad's Tibetsi mountains have been dated to the so-called Age of Hunters, around 6,000 BC. As revealed by the magnificent paintings at Tassili, now in southern Libya, the central Sahara was once a thriving paradise of species and wetlands. Some finely incised etchings are wonderfully realistic, others almost modern in their looping lines and distorted planes. A remarkable one on the Messak plateau in Libya shows a jackal-headed man following an elephant, picking up and licking its dung – presumably a shaman accessing elephant power.

Rock art is not confined to Europe and Africa: Asia also has its examples, of almost equal antiquity, though elephants seem more sparse. A particularly strange one was recorded by one Dr K. Kamat, in a cave at Bhimbekata near Bhopal, showing an

This San elephant painting near Lake Chivero, Zimbabwe, is probably associated with 'rain-snake' motifs and fertility rituals.

unmistakable elephant contained within the womb of some kind of antelope – the remnant, perhaps, of some long-lost folk tale. Much later, from the second century BC onwards, Buddhists hollowed out the monastic caves of Ajanta in the gorge of the Waghora river, north-eastern Deccan plateau, and decorated the walls richly with depictions of, amongst other sensuous scenes, their Prince Siddhartha and of a playful white elephant, its trunk holding a lotus blossom. This image was later adopted as the logo for India's Tourism Department.

Asia's great artistic gift to the world is the art produced within the last 2,000 years, much of it associated with its religions, primarily Hinduism and Buddhism. These works have to count amongst the most ornate and vivid in human history. Some of the works arose from the myths of world origins, which are both variable and fantastic. The elephant has a key role to play.

In some of the earliest Hindu myths, the Creator cracks open the cosmic egg: its yolk forms the sun, the other contents the land, sea and sky. The two halves of the eggshell are then presented to a conclave of twelve sages, who chant as the world

An elephant rock engraving on the Djado plateau of north-west Niger, possibly 5,000 years old.

is formed. From the half in the Creator's right hand emerge eight tuskers (*diggaja*), four of which will take their place as pillars at the corners of the universe. The others include the magnificent Airvata, who will carry the god Indra, Lord of the Universe, about his business. (This scheme has been whimsically parodied by Terry Pratchett in his Discworld novels, in which four elephants teeter atop a celestial turtle.) Indra was associated above all with thunder and the life-giving rain. Hence, again and again in Indian literatures, the elephant is associated with water, the colour of its skin with the dark grey of monsoon clouds, thunder with the unpredictable rages of musth. A Sanskrit poet, Nilikantha, described an elephant in musth as 'filled with

'The Pregnancy':
rock art from
Bhimbekata, India,
possibly 20,000
years old, as
rendered by
Dr K. Kamat.

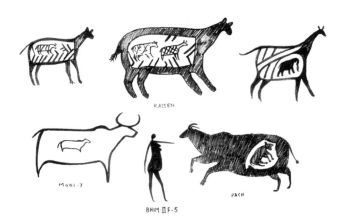

thunder like a rolled-up cloud'.[3] In their early existence, according to another story, elephants could fly about and even change shape as wilfully as clouds. Unfortunately, they once decided to land *en masse* on the branch of a banyan tree, which broke beneath their weight and flattened the hovel of a famed ascetic, Dirghatapas. Furious at being disturbed, he cursed them to gravity's pull and a role as man's beast of burden. In an epic poem of around AD 400, Kalidisa's *Meghaduta* ('The Cloud Messenger'), a banished *yaksha* or forest dweller, whose lord's garden has been trampled by an elephant while he was entwined in distracting love, calls on an elephant-shaped cloud for help:

The Hindu god
Indra mounted
on his elephant
Airvata, northern
India, 19th century.

> Exiled in the forest, love-starved, emaciated by denial,
> The *yaksha* lets a golden bracelet slip from off his listless
>   arm,
> And as the final days of summer draw to an end, he sees
>   a cloud,
> Like a musth bull elephant rutting against the moun-
>   tainside . . . [4]

68

Red elephant
outline on the
Jain temple at
Sravanabelagola,
India

The cloud, as elephant, then follows instructions to find the
yaksha's wife, drinking and spraying the world with rain as he
flies. Hence the association of the elephant with fecundity in
many forms.

Both the *Ramayana* and the *Mahabharata*, the great Sanskrit
epics of the first millennium BC, contain numerous elephant
stories derived from obscure folklore and mingled with practical
management techniques. There, too, the turmoil of the world,
figured in the exile of Rama and Sita to the forest, involves an
elephant – in this case, the accidental killing of a young ascetic,
mistaken in darkness for an elephant, by Rama's father
Dashartha. Although, as we have seen, Ganesh emerged under
Aryan influence rather late in the process, the myth nevertheless
arose that the *Mahabharata* had been written by the elephant-
headed god Ganesh himself, using his solitary tusk as a pen.

The legends related about Ganesh's origins are many, but
here is one: Ganesh was the son of Shiva, the cosmic mover,
and his gorgeous wife Parvati. They had struggled to conceive,
despite Shiva being incited to desire by the flowery arrow of

Kama, god of love. In musth, as it were, Shiva once displeased Parvati by surprising her at her bathing. So Parvati scraped the dirt from her body, mixed it with oil and secret ingredients, and moulded Ganesh from it. Set to guard her bathroom door, Ganesh barred Shiva on his next visit – at the cost of having his head lopped off by the furious god. So stricken was Parvati that a contrite Shiva sent messengers to bring the first replacement head they could find. It 'just happened' to be an elephant.

The details of Ganesh's appearance in countless votive statues and paintings are equally rich in mythology. He lost one tusk in a fight with Parasa-Rama, an incarnation of Vishnu the destroyer. He rides on a rat, who helps him in more subtle ways to remove obstacles – his main job in life. His corpulent belly suggests both affluence and power. He is always depicted holding symbolic objects: a whip, a lotus, a radish or a death's head. Ganesh or

Two images of Ganesh, the most popular of all the Hindu gods: a painting, and a modern Ganesh rendered in metal, looking like a cross between a bulldog and a Hell's Angel.

Ganesa became, and remains to this day, the most popular of all the teeming Hindu pantheon of gods and goddesses. He became known, in short, as 'Lord of Beginnings, Undertakings and Examinations' and the 'Remover of Obstacles'.

He even found his way into Buddhist lore, sometimes conflated with Indra's sacred mount as the pachyderm responsible for the birth of the Buddha himself. Buddha (born as Siddhartha), son of a noble from Kapilavastu, died a normal human death around 483 BC; but the myths that grew up around him figured him as one of a series of reincarnated Enlightened Ones, and he was born, like Christ, to a virgin, the Queen Sirimahamaya. She herself, though beautiful, with 'arms more lithe than an elephant's trunk', had devoted herself to

Some of the famous Thai royal 'white elephants', photographed by William Henry Jackson in the late 19th century.

chaste austerity. But one night in her Himalayan palace (she claimed), a 'silvery-white elephant descended from the mountains, entered my room and bowed down before me. In its trunk it bore a lotus. I was awakened by the call of a bird.' And so, impregnated by the visitor's trunk, she retired to the Lumbini Garden to give birth to the Buddha.

Ganesh images apart, Buddhist lore exhibits a culture deeply familiar with elephants: the *Jataka* stories – folk tales that relate the Buddha's previous births and lives – are full of stories of elephants in captivity and war. One story is particularly poignant: the enlightened Buddha, or Bodhisattva, is reincarnated as a wild elephant with blind parents, to whom he is devoted. Captured by a hunter and taken to the local king of

Marble elephants at Nemnath Temple, Mt Abu, India, photographed *c.* 1903.

Elephant statues line the Avenue of Spirits leading to the Ming tombs outside Beijing, carved in 1435.

Benares, he pines; the king, alert to distress, releases him to be reunited with his bereft parents. Often, it seems, there is in these tales a wealth of observed, even scientific, knowledge; a capacity to cross an uneasy border from human to elephant; and a willingness to learn from elephant family mores. It was primarily Buddha's incarnation into the wisest and most munificent of all beasts that prompted the ongoing worship of the white elephant, especially in Thailand: 'Mouth open, head the colour of cochineal, tusks gleaming like silver, all aglitter with precious stones, clad in the finest of golden tulle, his limbs and organs were flawlessly proportioned, his bearing majestic.'[5]

Hence, throughout Hindu and Buddhist Asia, the elephant features prominently in religious iconography, sometimes uneasily coalescing with royal or aristocratic power. Innumerable temples and palaces are guarded by massive colonnades of elephants: at the Wodeyar palace in Mysore; at the Maharana Palace at Udaipur, overlooking the waters of India's Lake Pichola;

at the Kailasantha Temple at Ellora. There is a magnificent blue beast in front of the temple of Bodnath in Nepal; another accompanied by two calves in Ayuthya, Thailand's former capital; another before the Pura Puseh temple in Batubulan, Bali. The second-century BC Ruanweli Dagoba palace in Sri Lanka is surrounded by rows of life-size, sanguine-looking elephants; the walls of Angkhor Wat in Cambodia bulge with elephant friezes. Most impressively, perhaps, kneeling elephants guard the so-called Avenue of Spirits leading to the Ming tombs near Beijing in China, built around 1435.

Islam, with its general reticence towards representational art, seems not to have depicted many elephants. Not that they were ignored: Alfred Edmund Brehm, author of an immense nineteenth-century study of animals, wrote: "'Elephants will leave you alone if you don't bother them,' a sheikh once told me on the banks of the Blue Nile. 'They left my father alone and his father before him. When the monsoon season is nigh, I hang amulets on tall poles; for these righteous animals, that is enough. They revere the word of Allah's prophet! They fear the retribution that awaits blasphemers. They are righteous animals".'[6]

Egyptian amulet in serpentine and bone inlay; late Naqada II, c. 3500-3300 BC, height 3.5 cm.

A seventh-century statue from Kashan in Persia depicts large round shields over the elephant's ears, a driver and two lovers, perhaps, under an exaggerated howdah canopy. And the elephant commands a special place in an extravagantly illustrated thirteenth-century Arabic bestiary, the *Manifiʾal-Hajawan* – 'On the Use of Animals'. (The author claimed that elephants lived for 400 years and that ivory powder cured leprosy.)

In ancient Egypt, despite the presence of both live elephants and a lot of worked ivory (notably a headrest from Tutankhamun's tomb in the form of the sun god Shu), elephants seem not to have featured much in the hieroglyphic art of the dynastic periods. There are some representations, however, that show a clear distinction between domesticated and wild elephants. The Metropolitan Museum of Art possesses an exquisitely simple artefact that is at once two elephants and a single face, in serpentine with bone-inlay eyes, dating from late Naqada II, around 3600 BC. The black obelisk of Shalmaneser III (858–824 BC) at Nimrud depicts a rather crude elephant with an oddly tiny head, being stiffly pursued by a man with a human-headed dog (or lion?) on a leash. And in 1667 the sculptor Bernini used an Egyptian feature in mounting an already ancient obelisk, originally erected by the Romans in honour of the goddess Minerva, atop a recognizably Asian elephant, for a monument to stand before the Roman church of Santa Maria sopra Minerva. Sixty years later, the architect Giovanni Battista Vaccarini imitated Bernini: he purloined a pink marble obelisk, made in Aswan and up to then a finishing post for races in the circus of the Italian town of Catania, and mounted it on an elephant carved from volcanic tufa in the Roman era. The monument's nickname in the Sicilian language is 'Liotru', a reference to Elidoros, a heretical eighth-century apostate and wizard who sought, through magic, to make the stony elephant walk. As

James V. Lafferty's elephant-shaped building, affectionately known as 'Lucy', Margate City, New Jersey.

76

one website drily notes, 'There's no evidence that his attempts met with any success.' But it remains the centrepiece of Catania's Piazza Duomo.

A little further south, the Sudan has contributed some early, sketchy engravings, an evidently domesticated and adorned elephant on the frieze of the Lion Temple at Musaw-warat (first century AD), and the intriguing, blocky 'elephant colossus' in red sandstone at the same place. (This house-sized statue is something of a precursor, perhaps, to more whimsical modern 'elephant buildings', like the Lucy Hotel built in South Atlantic City in the 1880s by Philadelphia engineer and speculator James V. Lafferty, and Bangkok's 'Chang' – Thai for elephant – building.) Clearly the elephant acted as a symbol of royal power and prestige, though whether it was revered amongst the Sudanese in any religious fashion remains unclear.

Sub-Saharan Africa to some extent continued the traditions of honouring and depicting elephants begun by the Stone Age ancients, though more recent African art is overwhelmingly anthropocentric. There are vastly fewer free-standing animal figures than human, though animal motifs are ubiquitously featured on human figurines and ritual objects. Elephant motifs appear on stools and masks, flywhisks and drums, tobacco pipes and calabashes. This is an aspect neglected by most accounts: Richard Carrington's 1958 classic *Elephants* offers a few pages, but only to be disparaging of the customary tales of elephants as 'rather pointless and inconsequential' and illustrative of 'the childlike naïveté of the African mind'.[7] Even Martin Meredith's comprehensive-sounding book, *The African Elephant: A Biography*, contains scarcely a word about Africans' own cultural attitudes towards elephants before European colonization. One has to turn to Albert Jeannin's *L'Eléphant d'Afrique* for a more comprehensive survey.

Elephants, unsurprisingly, often symbolized power. Doran Ross, in a catalogue for an exhibition, *Elephant*, held at the University of California's Fowler Museum in 1992, notes that some forty African cultures use elephant imagery. Many of their ritualistic significances remain jealously hidden from outsiders even today, as Canadian filmmaker Douglas Curran has noted of the great ceremonies of Malawi's Nyau people. One ceremony is dominated by a four-man elephant figure – the 'elephant with four hearts', it's called – and Curran rather despondently muses that even as the full meaning remains obscure, the culture of the Nyau (meaning 'mask') is itself on the verge of annihilation in today's globalizing world.[8]

We know some things. Not unlike the Buddhists, some Africans believed that their chiefs were reincarnated as elephants. At Igbo Ukwu in Nigeria in the tenth century the leader was buried with his feet resting on elephant tusks. For various clans, the elephant became a totem and the clans took their name: the Ndovu among the Bapimbwe in Tanzania, the Ndlovu in Zimbabwe. The Zulu chieftains, from Shaka in the early nineteenth century onwards, have styled themselves 'Great Elephant'. To this day, the Lozi of northern Zambia carry their king to coronation on a multi-oared boat, the *nalik-wanda*, adorned with an elephant figure. In West Africa, thrones and altars might be flanked by carved or plain elephant tusks. One of the Ashanti or Asante of Ghana royalty's main insignia was the Golden Elephant's Tail (*Sika mmara*). Leather from elephant skin might be sewn into the soles of Danhome kings' sandals, to impart their *bo* or spiritual power as evoked by art. There is no record of Africans taming elephants until the twentieth century (though one ivory carving seems to show a king astride one). But if you couldn't sit on a real jumbo, you could at least sit on a carving: the *asantahene*,

Nigerian bronze group.

Wooden Benin hip-mask; the trunk ends in a human hand.

Wood carving by an unknown Makonde artist, northern Mozambique.

Asante kings, alone were permitted to perch on a wooden stool carved as an elephant.

(This sort of thing was not confined to Africa: one Romualdus carved a throne for Bishop Urso of Canosa in the eleventh century, ornamented in the Byzantine style, which was supported by two elephants. Poor 'Sulayman' was an elephant given by John III of Portugal to the upcoming Austro-Hungarian emperor Maximilian in 1552. Having endured a gruelling trek from Genoa to Vienna, Sulayman died exhausted a year later, and then suffered a further indignity: two of his leg bones and a shoulder blade were fashioned by the mayor of Vienna into a gruesome chair, exhibited at the Benedictine chapter house in Krems Cathedral.)

Though rare, examples of carved elephants from pre-colonial Africa do exist. One unusual bronze group from Nigeria consists of two men with handaxes following or herding two bug-like little elephants with hands on the ends of their trunks – possibly intended for sacrifice. In the Hamburg Museum is an 8-inch- (20 cm-) high waist mask from Benin. It is a stylized elephant face with a hand at the trunk's tip, symbolizing its dexterity. Many parts of the continent lack a long tradition of sculpture, and we have to come down to the modern period, when the whole concept of an independent 'African art' becomes problematic. African artists and Picasso, for example, are variously said to have been borrowing from each other. Some recent sculpture, then, seems remarkably Cubist or Surrealist, though it often draws also on local folklores. Increasingly, what were once innovative motifs created by excellent individual sculptors (at one point in the 1990s, three of the four greatest stone sculptors in the world were said to be Zimbabwean Shona artists) shade off into the derivative, mass-produced little soapstone and wood carvings sold to tourists along Africa's roadsides.

A fantasial elephant from a late-12th-century bestiary.

For a long time after the implosion of the Roman Empire, as we've already noted, Europe lost much of its global contact, and at least as far as the elephant was concerned fell into a strangely timeless zone of ignorance. Depictions of elephants in bestiaries, illuminated manuscripts and cathedral sculptures through the

The unusually accurate depiction of the elephant given by Louis IX of France to Henry III of England in 1254/5 for his menagerie in the Tower of London, was apparently drawn from the life by Matthew Paris, though there are different versions. This watercolour is from the *Chronica Maiora*.

Middle Ages become conventionalized into anatomically inaccurate fantasy creatures – a far cry from the exquisitely observed Roman mosaics from Tunisia or Sicily, say, which included elephants fighting lions and crossing man-made trellis bridges. The second-century *Physiologus*, widely disseminated for more than a millennium, depicts elephants with tusks like a boar's, droopy trumpet-like trunks and bodies like cattle or horses. (According to the text, they couldn't breed without eating mandrake fruit.) This European image seems drawn from more ancient Northern sources, such as the Gunderstrup Cauldron from Denmark. Its fantastical spotted elephants in beaten silver and gold plate lope along above some bird-headed, winged and taloned lion-like creatures. This crudely drawn, bovine-hoofed and trumpet-trunked 'elephant' was slavishly copied down the centuries, as in a twelfth-century illuminated manuscript showing two complacent, donkey-sized elephants being bloodily speared in the chest by armoured riders, and a rather smug fourteenth-century carving loftily adorning Reims Cathedral (the elephant was a common motif amongst the stonemasons of Gothic churches). The

An absurd representation of Hanno, with Emanuel I of Portugal (1469–1521) precariously mounted. Hanno was given away to Pope Leo X in 1515.

Martin Schöngauer's famous engraving of 1480.

latter, at least, now has decent elephantine feet and ears clearly derived from an Asian exemplar.

Indeed, as the first individual elephants, usually gifts amongst kings, began to reappear in central and western Europe, more anatomically accurate depictions followed. One was that by Johannes de Cuba of Strasbourg, illustrating the 'Horus Sanitatis' of 1483; another was by Leonardo da Vinci. At the same time – even as the famous emperor Akbar in India was commissioning miniature battle scenes involving highly accurate and colourfully adorned elephants with slightly but deliberately caricatured features – European illustrators seemed to embark on another convention: an Asian-based but grossly distorted elephant with an enormous head, lots of fine bristles and widely spaced eyes looking almost straight ahead. This was a mode that persisted, despite the increasing evidence of its inaccuracy, right into the nineteenth century, and indeed into some modern kitsch.

By and large, however, the explosion of post-Renaissance empirical science, the increasing presence of actual elephants in zoos and royal menageries, and burgeoning travel by Europeans to both Asia and Africa, meant that elephants were ever more accurately portrayed. The first known dissection of an elephant in the West occurred in Dundee in 1706: a doctor worked while militia stopped the crowds going off with bits of the carcass, an event brought to life in Andrew Drummond's novel of 2008, *Elephantina*. Hundreds of black-and-white etchings and illustrations accompanied the many European hunters' accounts that emerged from colonial explorations. Once it became clear in the nineteenth century that elephants were being shot to the point of extinction, painting pictures of them increasingly became an act of tribute and later even a means of fundraising for elephant conservation. Such wildlife artists have now proliferated into

Two examples of modern kitsch, showing African and European artistic conventions.

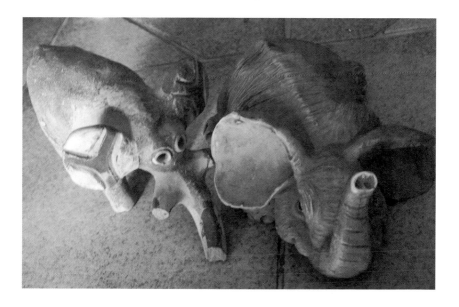

the hundreds, but none has been more active in promoting the elephant cause through his painting than David Shepherd OBE. Calling himself in his autobiography *The Man Who Loves Giants* (the other giants he loves to paint are steam engines), Shepherd raised £100,000 for conservation just at his 70th birthday bash in 2001. His oil painting, *Wise Old Elephant,* must be the single most widely reproduced elephant portrait of recent times.

If Shepherd represents a near-photographic realist end of the Western painting spectrum, Salvador Dalí must represent the opposite: the elephants that march in from the stormy horizon in *The Temptation of St Anthony* (1946) do so on the most spidery of legs, and bear monumental 'howdahs' that are a mix of motifs taken from Byzantine cathedrals, Botticelli nudes and an obelisk-like defensive tower. Quite different but just as nightmarish is Max Ernst's *The Elephant of Celebes* (1921), which is apparently an assemblage of machine parts, with flexible black ducting for a trunk and a bull's head. Evidently at least some artists' penchant for the fantastical has remained constant, from pre-Christian Norseland to ancient Ghana to twentieth-century Parisian studios. And the elephant always has potential to inspire a strangely discomforting awe.

Written literature depicting the elephant is, not surprisingly, as diverse as painting and sculpture. From the ancient Vedic epics of early India, through folk tales, parables and adages in almost every culture, to modern poems and novels, elephants appear everywhere. Power, magnificence, memory, familial relations – these are the major motifs. Where African cultures have handed down wisdoms in their proverbs, using elephants as an image, the tone is usually respectful at least. Here are some Shona proverbs from Zimbabwe:

An elephant with calves does not cough up phlegm.
One who is holding a treasure does not expose it to
 danger.

An elephant is taboo in public but in private is delicious.
Hypocrites pretend to be of good character but reveal
 loose morals under cover of privacy.

An elephant is not burdened by its own tusks.
One should be equal to one's own responsibilities.

The elephant died on account of the ant.
A small habit, left uncontrolled, can harm the whole
 community.[9]

A Malawian friend told me this one: *From the back of an elephant you cannot see the dew* – meaning, don't lose the bigger picture in attention to trivial detail. There are hundreds more examples, but here's the most famous of all, applicable to so many situations and so widespread in Africa that its origins are lost: *When two elephants fight, it is the grass that suffers.*

There are such proverbs in all cultures. An Indian one: *Only an elephant can bear an elephant's load.* From Sri Lanka: *The elephant does not see with its own eyes how big it is* and *Lost opportunities cannot be drawn back even by the might of elephants.* From Italy: *Even if your enemy is an ant, see in him an elephant.* And of course the US adage, 'See the elephant in the room' – that which is ignored but ultimately unavoidable. I recently heard Al Gore use this with reference to global warming sceptics.

But elephants are also often seen as a threat, especially when, as in many parts of Africa and Asia, the local humans are none too well equipped to fend them off. Some of this fearfulness is conveyed by this section of a Nigerian Yoruba poem, 'The Elephant', written by E. A. Babalola in somewhat archaic English in 1954:

> He breathes gracefully and with dignity.
> He walks gracefully and with dignity.
> He is distinguished by his bulky tail.
> To tie him to a stake is impossible.
> The Oba [chieftain] who will tie him so is still to reign.
> In the jungle, as well as in the bush,
> He makes a fire to warm himself and feels at home.
> The treading of a single elephant
> Makes all the forest trees both big and small
> To shake from their top to their very roots.
> His is ne'er the shame of suffering hunger

In his forest home; for he wards that off
By letting loose his anger on the forest trees,
And thus to them he proudly shifts the shame.[10]

The elephant could also be depicted as lacking in a certain acuity. The Duiker is frequently said to have outwitted the giant. Another common African folk tale (parallelled, interestingly, by similar stories from India) tells of how the Hare tricked the Elephant out of being elected King of the Animals. As Hare's village happened to be on the way to the gathering-place for the great election, he hung about until Elephant came through. Hare collapsed on the ground, all bulging eyes and racked breath, barely able to croak out a request that the Elephant carry him to the meeting. Elephant, naturally compassionate, lifted Hare onto his back. When they reached the gathering, Hare's illness instantly vanished, he preened and waved to the crowds – and since it was he who rode even above the mightiest of beasts, Hare was the one who was invested with the title. Such tales bear endless repetition: just one, 'Why Elephant and Hyena Live Far From People', is retold by Alexander McCall Smith, better known for quirky Botswana-set detective novels.[11]

Other traditional oral literature could take a more compassionate view. A Hurutshe poem from northern South Africa is a remarkable reversal of the usual stereotypes and a feeling of real identity with the elephant, who narrates the poem:

I'm the big one of the mother of trees,
The big one eating trees,
Picker of leaves,
Big-grain-basket of the hyena's place,
Worm with the big appetite,
Digger of trees:

The Syrischer Maler woodcut print, Syria, c. 1354, illustrating an originally Indian folktale of Fairuz the Hare and the Elephant.

Let me dig the shepherd's tree and the *elandsboontjie*.
I'm the big one of the mother of trees.
I'm the elephant, kin to mankind,
Hence I regard mankind's ways with fear;
And so, when I kill one, I bury him, like people do,
And I stay unmarried, like people do,
And I rub on medicine, like people do.
I'm the big one of the mother of trees,
Smasher of trees.[12]

Alternatively, they could be commemorated as a resource, as in this verse from a traditional African song:

Hunter of elephants, take your bow!
In the forest where nothing passes by but you,
Hunter! Lift your head, glide, run, leap and walk.
Your meat lies before you, an immense slab of meat,

Meat that walks like a mountain,
Meat that makes the heart rejoice.
Meat you'll roast in your hearth,
Meat in which you'll sink your teeth,
Beautiful, red meat whose blood is drunk steaming . . . [13]

This is at least celebratory. The literature of another kind of
hunter altogether – the European 'sportsman' and ivory hunter
– was murderous. These gentlemen spawned an extensive genre
of hunting literature, the conventions of which fed off each
other until by the late nineteenth century a major publishing
industry had developed around the genre. Many accounts
related the endless slaughter of Africa's elephants. William
Finaughty, William Cornwallis Harris, Roualeyn Cumming,
Arthur Neumann, Frederick Courteney Selous – these were
among the names all but revered by subsequent hunters. They
established the style of the genre. They made a virtue of their
apparent roughness and routinely expressed humbleness at
the shortcomings of their literary skills, but in fact were often
canny writers who knew exactly what they were doing. The
following passage from Neumann's *Elephant Hunting in East
Equatorial Africa* (1898) must serve as an example of their kind
of prose, and of the militaristic precision with which they
narrated their hunts:

The breeze being happily favourable for once, I got up
close without much difficulty, and made out two or three
enormous bulls standing together. One faced me, another,
whose tusks (from the glimpse I got) seemed as good,
stood broadside on. By great good luck I could see the
vulnerable part of his ribs, just behind his shoulder,
through a little opening among the leaves, etc., and was able

An elephant hunt
in Brazza, Congo,
in 1887.

to get a shot by kneeling. Following, as they disappeared
instantly after I fired, there was just a colour of blood (a
very spot or two only); and, though I felt positive my aim
had been true, I began to fear another failure. But, just

after, he was heard ahead, and a little way on we came up to him standing in a little bare place. I gave him two more shots and he toppled over.[14]

And you will find screeds more of this depressing, essentially uninformative stuff, leavened only by observations about local peoples and customs in the explorer mode. By the time of Neumann's writing, though, a consciousness that other opinions were current is palpable, and these hunter-writers are often quite defensive about their task. But many features of their style continue to make their presence felt in more recent hunting literature, and even in the self-deprecating, laconic but macho prose of the newer genre of game-ranger memoirs. Being chased by an angry elephant is, of course, a staple of such reminiscences, as is the image of the so-called 'rogue elephant' – actually usually suffering from some human-inflicted wound or something as banal as toothache.

The earliest forays towards scientific collecting amongst some nineteenth-century 'sportsmen' (Selous took home innumerable 'specimens' for English museums), their familiarity with the animals and growing guilt at their own depredations, gradually transmuted into full-blown ethology or animal-behavioural studies and conservationists' accounts, which finally incorporated the language of ecology and biodiversity. These scientific perspectives have affected the prose of elephant managers' and biologists' more public literary works, though something gung-ho, however modified by regret, often remains in their general advocacy of 'culling' as a management tool.

Another minor literary industry has developed around elephant-focused memoirs, written by those who love African elephants most: Cynthia Moss, Daphne Sheldrick, the Douglas-Hamiltons, Richard Leakey, Joyce Poole, Katy Payne, David

Paynter and many others. These have been accompanied by an explosion of photographic coffee-table books and glossy wildlife magazines, stimulated at once by the development of ever more refined photographic equipment and the creation of the touristic wildlife park experience. Not only the tourist brochures, but also the photographic books have developed generic norms of their own, to the point of predictability. The photos themselves often sanitize the realities, concentrating on elephant familial relations, babies playing with their trunks and being rescued from mud, close-ups of wrinkled skin, solitary bulls silhouetted against dusty sunsets, etc., etc. It's sobering to return to a book like Peter Beard's *The End of the Game* (1965) with its grim assessment of human cruelty: page after page of shocking sepia aerial photos of elephant corpses, forming almost abstract montages, are the very antithesis of the colourful, calm, playful spreads that are the conventions of the coffee-table genre.

Novels about elephants were also spun out of the hunting genre, and many of them involved hunters. Henry Rider

Edward van Altena's photo of American president Theodore Roosevelt posing with his kill 'somewhere in Africa', c. 1909.

94

Haggard's African-set potboilers, *King Solomon's Mines* (1886) being only the most famous of them, took his character Allan Quartermain into the heart of elephant country, and established the norms for most of his successors. Ernest Hemingway was one such successor writer (though he hunted elephants in Kenya, his story 'Hills like White Elephants' doesn't actually have anything to do with the animals). Thriller writer John Gordon-Davis made a Hemingwayesque 'Great White Hunter' the central character in his popular 1975 novel, *Taller than Trees* (this being the name of a bull elephant with which the hunter has an old-fashioned, drawn-out duel – a translation of the Zulu name 'Dhlulamiti', an actual elephant who once haunted Kruger National Park).

In time, shifts in attitude towards a more compassionate conservation were also registered in fiction. Wilbur Smith's gore- and sex-sodden thrillers, while similar to Davis's, nevertheless begin to depict a new sensitivity towards elephants, as in the description of a culling scene in *Elephant Song* (1991). The man in charge, Johnny Nzou (his name 'by coincidence' means elephant in Shona, though the character is Zulu), expresses a deep repugnance for the killing his department is forced to undertake. The novel's hero, Daniel Armstrong, asks a provocative question: 'Your management of your herds of elephants has been too good . . . Now you have to destroy and waste these marvellous animals.' Nzou replies: 'No, we won't waste them. We will recover a great deal of value from their carcasses . . . The death of these animals will not be a complete abomination.' Nzou berates Armstrong for using 'the emotive, slanted language of the animal rights groups', reflecting the tension between scientific objectivity and rights-based 'emotionality' that indeed bedevils the elephant-management debates. But as the cull comes to an end, Nzou himself bids the dead matriarch farewell in quasi-religious terms: 'Go in peace,' he intones, 'and forgive us what we have done to your tribe'[15] – a gauche sort of African solidarity. The elephants rapidly disappear from the story, however, and Smith gets on with his usual globe-trotting harum-scarum adventures, with little further thought about conserving charismatic herbivores.

Much more central to the story are the elephants of another South African novel, Dalene Matthee's *Circles in a Forest* (1984). First written in Afrikaans, the story centres on a traditional woodcutter family living in an uneasy but deeply respectful symbiosis with the elephants of South Africa's Knysna forests. Before the timber and gold-panning industries devastated these huge yellow-wood forests in the early twentieth century, a substantial number of elephants lived there (they later virtually vanished, and only in 2007 did DNA sampling of dung deposits confirm that five highly secretive individuals survive). Saul Barnard, the novel's hero, has a profoundly knowledgeable and ecologically sensitive relationship with the forest and its huge inhabitants, especially the greatest bull, Old Foot, and this rather moving story narrates his largely futile attempts to save it all from over-exploitation and death.

> Since that first day when Old Foot stood in the open, he had dreamed up an imaginary bond between him and the elephant. When he became a man and his boyhood dreams began to blur, a feeling of respect, of an intense awareness of the old forest patriarch started taking the place of dreams. No, it was more. There was something between him and Old Foot that the most sober thinking could not always staunch.[16]

Even more central are the elephants of Canadian novelist Barbara Gowdy's *The White Bone* (1998), mentioned earlier. This is a beautifully written and sophisticated, if not wholly convincing, attempt to relate the world from the elephant's point of view, imagining a whole elephant history and culture, with its independent language, naming practices and memories transmitted down the generations. But it plays dangerously along that borderline where anthropomorphism – always a sticky point for the more scientific types – spills over into the improbable.

The elephant-as-speaker is more generally encountered in children's literature, where such fantasies are, for some reason, regarded as more legitimate. Of this literature there is a such an elephantine amount, from Disney's Dumbo to Dr Seuss's Horton to A. A. Milne's elusive heffalump, that I'll not even attempt to survey it here. But we can't pass over Babar, one of the most famous of all animal characters, and surely the most popular fictional elephant. Created in French by Jean du Brunhoff in 1931, the little elephant, after witnessing his mother's slaughter in Africa, finds his way to Paris, imbibes all the treasures of French civilization, including his trademark green outfit, and returns to Africa to persuade all his animal friends (literally) to follow suit. De Brunhoff wrote half a dozen stories before his premature death at the age of 37; his son Laurent has continued the line with at least twenty more since 1946. A movie was made in 1989; a TV series ran to 78 episodes and was screened in 150 countries; 12 million copies of the books have been sold; you can visit an online Babar Museum; and someone estimated that every second Japanese woman under 30 owns a Babar artefact. Babar-inspired music was composed by Francis Poulenc, amongst others. Most recently, Raphael Mostert, previously best known for music using Tibetan 'singing' bowls, has produced an opera for children based on the 1936 *Travels with Babar*, the second of the books (it premieres in 2008).

Babar the elephant, created by Jean du Brunhoff.

Babar is, in short, a household name, though you won't learn anything about real elephants from him. Some critics – the Chilean writer Ariel Dorfman for one – have condemned the Babar series as being politically offensive beneath its charming surface, foreshadowing if not justifying the ideology of neo-colonialism. Laurent de Brunhoff himself recognized this when he declined to reissue one of his father's more youthful, potentially racist stories. But Babar has been adopted by almost everyone else. The ever popular Enid Blyton produced an abridged version of the early stories in the middle of the Second World War: 'Enemy action', her editor noted, 'while destroying many less desirable records, has reduced to ashes a large proportion of those delightfully coloured sheets in which the genius of Jean de Brunhoff and the skill of the colour-printer had combined to immortalize his career. But Babar is not easy to blitz.'[17] Isabelle Chevrel, a lecturer at the University of Rennes, probably speaks for millions: Babar 'belongs to the universe of children through the innocence of his outlook and the supple roundness of his shape . . . His world is one of love and wisdom, poetry and nostalgia. It is closed, rich and reassuring.'[18] In the most recent incarnation, the rotund suited creature is *Babar le p'tit ecolo* – the little environmentalist, trying to make the world greener by avoiding deodorants.

To return to the world of adults, many more elephant novels exist, but the most frequently mentioned and anthologized has to be Romain Gary's *The Roots of Heaven* (originally *Les Racines du ciel*, 1956, written in French, though Gary was born in Lithuania). John Huston made a film of it in 1958. It's a curious tale, set in French Equatorial Africa at that time when the arrogance of hunting was clashing with new protectionist movements, and at times seems almost a kind of existentialist meditation rather than an elephant adventure. Morel, the hero, having failed to make headway with a petition to save the elephants, embarks on a crusade of low-grade terrorism to protect the precious animals against ivory poachers and hunters, getting mixed up with political rebels as he does so. Elephants, Morel tells a barmaid at one point, were 'the very image of immense liberty'. When he was a miserable prisoner of war in Germany, he goes on, he 'tried to think of those big animals marching irresistibly through the open spaces of Africa, and it made us feel better'. This doesn't quite gel with what Gary wrote in an introduction to the 1964 Time-Life reprint, but he nevertheless says a lot about the power of elephant lore:

... there has hardly been a critic who has not referred to *The Roots of Heaven* as a symbolic novel. I can only state firmly and rather hopelessly that it is nothing of the sort. It has been said that my elephants are really symbols of freedom, of African independence. Or that they are the last individuals threatened with extinction in our collective, mechanized, totalitarian society. Or that these almost mythical beasts evoke in this atheistical age an infinitely bigger and more powerful Presence. Or, then again, that they are an allegory of mankind itself menaced with nuclear extinction. There is almost no limit to what you can make an elephant stand for, but if the image of this lovable pachyderm thus becomes for each of us a sort of Rorschach test – which was exactly my intention – this does not make him in the least symbolic. It only goes to prove that each of us carries in his soul and mind a different notion of what is essential to our survival, a different longing and a personal interpretation, in the largest sense, of what life preservation is about.[19]

The Roots of Heaven won the coveted Prix Goncourt, and influenced at least some subsequent novels: Hammond Innes's *The Big Footprints* (1977), though set in the semi-desert of northern Kenya, reads very much like a less philosophical version of Gary's novel.

And of course in innumerable, unlisted examples that one will find only by pleasurable accident, the elephant will be used as a metaphor for something else. Here are just three examples from famous novels. In *Les Misérables* Victor Hugo described the people of Paris building 'an elephant forty feet high, made of scaffolding covered with masonry, carrying on its back a

Among innumerable novels, Jules Verne's *Cinq Semaines en Balon* (1863) features an elephant dragging his balloon along.

tower resembling a house', which stood as some 'sort of symbol of the popular force'.[20] Charles Dickens, in his great industrial-age critique *Hard Times*, described how the 'piston of the steam-engine worked monotonously up and down, like the head of an elephant in a state of melancholy madness';[21] and in Virginia Woolf's *The Waves*, a circus elephant is one character's image of constriction: 'The beast stamps; the elephant with its foot chained.'[22]

I have yet to find many novels dealing with elephants from Asia, although, given that India produces vast amounts of printed material, they surely exist in numbers. Among recent publications, a novel entitled *Ashes for the Elephant God*, by one Vijaya Shartz, has more to do with Ganesh than with elephants as such; Ashok Mathur's *Once Upon an Elephant* depicts the insertion of Ganesh worship into modern Indian immigrant communities in Canada; and Rajikha Rao's *The Elephant and the Maruti* is premised on an accidental collision between an elephant and a Maruti car, though again the animals aren't central. (The best-advertised Indian text at the time of writing is a non-fiction survey of modern India by novelist Shashi Tharoor, tellingly entitled *The Elephant, the Tiger and the Cell-Phone*.)

There is, however, a wonderful story in verse by Vikram Seth, best known for his gargantuan novel *A Suitable Boy*. It's a modern folk tale in rhyming couplets, in which a community of talking animals, led by the Tragopan – a species of pheasant – invade the office of the local human bigwig to protest against the planned building of a dam. There's a scuffle; the Tragopan dies tragically; and the elephant does little more than pour a pot of hot tea over the Great Bigshot. The tale deliberately refrains from pushing a single moral, though the ecological sensitivity is clear enough, and the elephant mourns that man

Stamps bear elephant images from the world over.

is paradoxically both 'mild and vicious', both 'sane and mad', ravaging the world in a state of 'uneasy selfishness'.[23]

There are any number of poems depicting the elephant, from the earliest Indian epics, the *Mahabharata* and the *Rig Veda*, to Heathcote Williams's illustrated eulogy. Few surveys of elephants omit Jonathan Swift's quip about imaginative cartographers popping in an elephant 'for want of towns' to fill an empty space, or John Donne's verse in *The Progress of the Soul* about 'Nature's master-peece, an Elephant, The onely harmlesse great thing'. Edward Lear's elephant portrait from 'An Animal Alphabet' is of course irresistible, just because it is so inconsequential:

> The Enthusiastic Elephant,
> who ferried himself across the water with the
> Kitchen Poker and a New Pair of Ear-rings.

But here are two less well-known, yet more substantial, southern African examples. Both take as their background the worldwide destruction of the elephant and its ultimate dependency on the whims of humans. Harold Farmer wrote his poem 'Absence of Elephants' in Zimbabwe; given the renewed upsurge in elephant-poaching there, it's unhappily prescient.

> Poems about elephants are better than elephants.
> Survival, what's that? The uprooting of trees, who cares?
> The slow, residual thickening of the forest floor
> with the accumulated detritus of elephants,
> the harried, panicky ants staring at logs in their path,
> the abrupt awakening of owls by crashing tusks,
> the collaboration upsetting the repose of the river,
> are only the outward and visible signs of the poem.
>
> The poem in the elephant is the breath of the elephant.
> Do elephants breathe? We never think of it like that,
> of the imperceptible suspiration of lesser beings.
> The elephants march through stanzas, cantos, epics.
> They dash their feet against the glossy, black boards

of continental circuses. 'Ah!' the crowd cries.
They take their place in the stone carvings of St Jerome,
and breathe a soft undertone to the sighs of worshippers.

The elephant is minister to the soul's grandeur . . . [24]

Rather more amusing, but no less disturbing in its implications,
is South African poet Douglas Livingstone's 'One Elephant':

About that time arose one elephant
from all the herd who stopped and cleared his throat
and said: I can't for all the world at all
remember what it was I had to say;
I only know it was of great importance.

He shook his ears; looked puzzled; slapped himself
with gusto on the back and raised the dust;
shifted capacious businessman's hindquarters
in their ill-fitting pants; harrumphed and glared
at the innocent thorn trees – his audience.

Ah yes! There comes a time when one commits,
despite oneself, the ultimate! And sick
of selfish beasts, their egos and their stench,
their cunning cruelty, destructivity,
one turns, despite oneself, grimly to Man . . . [25]

It's most fitting, perhaps, to end with a sobering extract from
Heathcote Williams's book *Sacred Elephant*. He ends his long
poem by asking how seeing the power of a real elephant affects
that age-old question, 'Who am I?'

In collaboration with their distant disposition,
A sense of their gathered power,
The child's awareness expands,
Before its attention is turned away
From the animal to the machine;
Before its passage is forced into a man-made society
With its elephantine surrogates:
Tower-blocks, juggernauts and trampling multinationals,
Monster markets, jumbo jets, and motorways . . .
Before it is crushed by the elephantiasis of technology,
Where there is less and less room for any mammals
Larger than rats.
And where, henceforth, the elephant may exist
Only in a scratched nature-film,
A destitute freak in a video zoo . . . [26]

Poetry is closely related to music, and elephants feature there, too – and not only the Thai Elephant Orchestra (we'll meet them again in chapter Four). Camille Saint-Saëns most famously incorporated the elephant into his *Carnival of the Animals*, though it was never performed before the composer's death in 1921. The Russian composer Igor Stravinsky collaborated in 1942 with choreographer George Balanchine to produce a ballet for 50 elephants for Balanchine's circus-owner friend John Ringling North. Nowadays, any number of more or less obscure music groups and businesses use the elephant name and image, only a few of which seem to have the welfare of elephants in mind. Some at least seem to have chosen the elephant as an icon of strong independence: the rock group Japonize Elephants from Bloomington, Indiana, is led by the idiosyncratically named 'Emperqq Zerlock'; the Czech musicians Pocket Elephants decline to submit to any label that might 'limit their illimitable souls and music feelings inconveniently';[27] and 'Elephants in the Room' deliberately broaches uncomfortable topics. But there's no coherence to be discerned in the welter of other appearances: among bands, labels and tracks you'll find elephants in Amsterdam, in the Attic, and in Love; Baby, Rushing, Frozen, Purple, White Onyx and Flying Pink elephants. You can fantasize about being 'Raped by Elephants'; relax with Hot Elephant Music's range 'E.A.S.Y.' (Even Elephants Are Sometimes Young); or mull over Andrea Shea's more politically conscious 'Where Elephants Weep', which refers to the horrific aftermath of Pol Pot's genocide in Cambodia.

Clearly here we are venturing – as Heathcote Williams warned – into that area of mass-produced meaninglessness that is the advertising industry and related commerce. (One blogger has even characterized 'evil advertisers' as 'the elephant in the room'!) Startling imagery is all. Owning a snapshot (or even better, posting a home-made video on YouTube) is more satisfying

Music and elephants often coincide; O. V. Schubert of Cleveland created this poster for the 'Original Georgia Minstrels' in 1876.

than actual experience. What might once have been uniquely significant examples of shamanistic rock art, like a Bushman cave painting, or of worshipful religious importance, like Ganesh in the Far East, have now proliferated through the touristic marketplaces into millions of cheap commercial baubles. I can go into the shop at my local Addo Elephant National Park, for example, and buy elephant images in the form of keyrings, mugs, T-shirts, caps, writing paper, postcards, postage stamps or DVDs, and figurines in blown glass, ceramic, grass, paper, wood, soapstone, steel, batik, watercolour or oil paint.

Even where elephants have never trodden earth, they pop up everywhere in advertising – nowhere more than in the US. The symbol of the Republican Party is only the most obvious one. Ironically, the same man invented the symbols for both main parties. Thomas Nast, in a cartoon that appeared in *Harper's Weekly* in 1874, drew a donkey clothed in a lion's skin, scaring away all the animals at the zoo. One of those animals, the elephant, was labelled 'The Republican Vote'. That's all it took for the elephant to remain associated with the Republican Party. Now, of course, they claim that it means strength and dignity.

Such associations are used in every imaginable field today. Just in my own area, I've noticed elephant symbolism used to push cement, a transport company, an estate agent, coach tours, an ale and heavy lifting equipment. The Elephanteria website lists dozens of uses of elephant imagery in advertising anything from printers to carpets, from silent floors to courier services – never advertising *elephants*, of course, but playing on the stereotypical attributes of flawless memory, strength, weight and reliability.[28]

Elephants, for obvious reasons, are often associated with enormous appetites, and are therefore used to advertise restaurants. Badly built statues of elephants clutter the entrances or interiors of diners across the United States, from 'Elephant Walk'

'Third-term panic': Thomas Nast's cartoon of 1874 inaugurated the elephant and donkey symbols for the main American political parties, to be reinforced by hundreds of cartoons down to the present.

in Boston to a pink extravagance in Shelton, Florida. Another pink elephant, this one plastic, adorns the Jumbo Liquor Store in Johannesburg's Hillbrow area, and is lampooned in Ivan Vladislavić 's novel *The Restless Supermarket:* its 'eyes like saucers, with painted pupils black as draughtsmen rattling in them', its 'pointed ears [that] stood on end like wistful wings'. As the novel opens, a drunk is trying to mount its 'shocking pink buttocks'.[29] No one seems quite sure why 'pink elephants' became associated with the hallucinations of drunkenness, but at least by 1913 Jack London could write in *John Barleycorn*:

> There are, broadly speaking, two types of drinkers. There is the man whom we all know, stupid, unimaginative, whose brain is bitten numbly by numb maggots; who walks generously with wide-spread, tentative legs, falls frequently in the gutter, and who sees, in the extremity of his ecstasy, blue mice and pink elephants. He is the type that gives rise to the jokes in funny papers.

Elephantine strength for a cement company. (The frond just discernible at the top is *Portulacaria*, a favourite elephant food.)

In 1932 Guy Lombardo had a popular hit with the song 'Pink Elephants', composed by Mort Dixon and Harry Woods:

Pink elephants on the table.
Pink elephants on the chair.
Pink elephants on the ceiling,
Pink elephants ev'rywhere.
Now I'm through making whoopee,
I raised my hand and swore
That I never intend to see
Those pink elephants any more.

As one commentator pointed out: 'It should be noted that the song also referred to a lavender alligator, a purple cow, a polka-dot boa constrictor, a beetle, a monkey, and a whippoorwill. But it was the pink elephant that stuck.'[30] Hence, probably, sundry beers feature elephants: amongst them Heiffer's from the US, Tusker from Kenya, Rogue from South Africa, Windhoek from Namibia, Elephant Stout from Singapore, Malt Liquor from Denmark. More sweetly, a well-known TV advert narrated how a little Indian boy created an 'elephant tower', using the elephants' alleged desire to drink Pepsi.

Apart from the contemporary cult of 'branding', film is undoubtedly the most powerful medium of our time. Elephants feature regularly in television advertising, too, at least in my part of the world in southern Africa, where real elephants are readily available for photoshoots. And, naturally, elephants have been an attractive subject, or just an accoutrement for screen goddesses and macho heroes alike, almost ever since film was possible. One website lists well over a hundred elephant films produced up to 2004, the earliest being *Frank Melville's Trick Elephant* of 1899.[31] This was made to sell Brothers's and

Forepaugh's circus, and showed an elephant walking over the prostrate bodies of two ponies. Such clips gave way to feature films. A quasi-documentary film by Merian C. Cooper and Ernest Schoedak, *Chang* (1927), set in Thailand, substituted rampaging elephants for the usual barbarian hordes: the animals end up captured and tamed. Robert Flaherty's *Elephant Boy* (1937) was based on Rudyard Kipling's story 'Toomai' from *The Jungle Book*. There was the 1954 *Elephant Walk*, featuring the sultry Elizabeth Taylor as wife of a tea baron in Ceylon, her illicit love playing out against the backdrop of 'the hovering, ominous menace of the hostile elephants' who have a 'grudge' against the plantation.[32] More ecologically sensitive to elephants was one of Clint Eastwood's less well-known directing-acting efforts, the 1990 *White Hunter, Black Heart*. Based on a book by Peter Viertel, it's a thinly disguised account of director John Huston and *his* making of *The African Queen* in 1951. In Eastwood's retelling, the director character is consumed by a desire to kill a particular tusker; he eventually decides not to shoot it, but with tragic results. Both films were shot in

Amarula Cream liqueurs are made from marula fruits, which are also choice elephant snacks.

Zimbabwe, and Eastwood reused the same little steamboat that Huston had. The tusker was 'acted' by a wild elephant living in Matusadona National Park in the north of the country.

And of course there are dozens of children's films and animated cartoons, following the lead of Disney's *Dumbo* of 1941. David Lynch's black-and-white film *Elephant Man* (1980), incidentally, had nothing to do with elephants, beyond the allegedly elephant-like appearance of poor John (in real life Joseph) Merrick's hideously wrinkled and bulbous medical condition, and the appalling manner in which he was displayed as a circus freak.

India produces more feature films than any other nation on earth, so it's not surprising to find elephantine examples among them. They often appeared in earlier mythological or historical movies, but gained greater prominence in 1971, in *Hathi Mera Sathi* ('My Companion the Elephant'). The young protagonist Raju, played by Rajesh Khanna, is repeatedly rescued by elephants – they chase off a leopard, engineer the central love-match by towing a broken-down car, help Raju work his way out of poverty by performing stunts, fetch a doctor, and one finally sacrifices its life by taking a bullet intended for Raju.[33] A celebrated filmmaker from Kerala, N. Balan, made a film called *The Eighteenth Elephant* (2003), which lamented the destruction of his region's elephants. And we can end a little heart-warmed by the film *Larger Than Life* (1996), in which a vagrant acquires an elephant and walks it home from America to Thailand.

Finally, there are documentaries now too numerous to encompass here. Cynthia Moss's films of *Echo of the Elephants*, the matriarch of her Kenyan study, have to count as hugely influential pioneers in the field. There has been *Africa: Kingdom of the Elephants*, National Geographic's *Reflections on Elephants* and *Elephant Rage*, David Malakoff's *The Urban Elephant* (about Bangkok's elephant orphans), Angela Bassett's *Whispers: An*

A stylized 'T' from Kipling's *Jungle Book.*

A window card for the motion picture, derived from Edgar Rice Burroughs's famous Tarzan novel, c. 1921.

Elephant's Tale, and many others. Now the techniques of the genre have become so sophisticated that we can view an elephant baby alive in its mother's womb; or, in another venture, from a camera hidden in a strategically placed elephant turd (at least one bull sensed a problem and booted the offending instrument into the nearby river). Probably no medium has been so influential in forming environmental attitudes globally, but I know of no study of elephant documentaries that might begin to gauge this. And even if we can know and understand elephants through film better than ever before, nothing can substitute for seeing them in person, as it were, in their natural spaces, or at least such spaces as we have contrived to leave to them. So in the final chapters we can turn from art back to life, and explore the realities of elephant lives and conservation today.

4 Using Elephants

'An elephant mounted by a king is radiant; a king mounted on an elephant is resplendent . . . Thus elephants should be protected like the life of a king.'[1]

So ran an early Indian book of elephant lore. The symbiosis between elephant and ruler implied there is not necessarily untrue, but humans have generally protected elephants only in order to use them in some way, and have generally used them only in order to glorify themselves. This has, broadly speaking, not been to the elephants' benefit: panic captures, hurtful taming, terror in the front line of battles, appalling sea journeys, stifling cages, confrontations with tigers, demeaning performances in unnatural postures, the drudgery of logging operations – this has been the lot of most captive elephants. Little of this has visibly bettered the fate of those few left in the wild. Perhaps only in the modern era of conservation have those glorified zoos, the game reserves, allowed elephants to approximate a natural life while still earning their human captors revenue.

Not that compassion and caring have been totally absent from human–elephant relations. Deep mutual affection, admiration, even reverence, is a persistent thread in a 5,000-year-old history – but there is almost always the underbelly of chains and cages, the sharp ankush or bullhook tugging at ear or foot to direct movement, the final glum submission.

On the ninth day of the Desara festival when Hindus honour their animals, to see an elephant advancing down a New Delhi street all but invisible under caprisons of extravagant gold, festooned in damask and copper bells, painted in fantastic patterns, its tusks ringed in silver – is to wonder whether the elephant is really being honoured in itself, or is merely being used as a canvas for human art.

Some uses require an elephant to be both alive and (or then) dead. When a hunter thrills in his chase – it is almost always 'his', testing his manhood and valour by confronting the greatest of all land mammals – it is only to prove that valour by killing it. Bits of dead elephant provide the boastful evidence: ivory carvings, a foot made into an umbrella stand or, in one of

An extravagantly adorned elephant with howdah.

the more grotesque examples, a whole preserved ear, painted with a charging elephant, mounted amongst United States presidents' memorabilia (see the website tellingly addressed hailtothechiefs.com). 'Abysmal kitsch', one writer called it. Dead, of course, elephants have always provided meat, hides and – pre-eminently – ivory. But in this chapter I want to focus on the utilization of living elephants.

We have evidence of the taming of elephants almost from the beginning of powerful civilizations: elephants as symbols of royal and imperial power; as weapons in wars and hunts; as pack animals, logging workers and bridge-builders; as entertainers in games, zoos and circuses; most recently, as semi-wild spectacles for tourists. As early as 3000 BC the Egyptians, presumably using the African elephants that ranged across North Africa until hunting and the desertification of the Sahara eliminated them, were fashioning hieroglyphs that distinguished between wild and trained elephants. A Sumerian terracotta carving representing an elephant with rider dates from 2000 BC. Contemporary with Sumer and Babylon, at Mohenjodharo and Harappa in Pakistan's Indus Valley, an advanced urban civilization was using trade seals carved in steatite. One shows an elephant clearly bearing a saddle-cloth.

The elephant is unlikely to have played a major role in these earliest societies. However, by the time the Aryans arrived in northern India, invading from the steppes of Turkestan in waves between 2000 and 1700 BC, they found in places a well-developed culture of elephant taming. This did not include domestication: there appears never to have been a programme of captive breeding, losses being replaced by new captures from the still-extensive wild populations. The evidence surfaces mainly in the books of the *Vedas*, a series that continued to be produced between 1200 and 600 BC, the *Ramayana*, the *Mahabharata* and the *Jataka* stories. Prior to the first millennium BC the chronology of these books remains obscure and the documentation occasionally controversial. However, it seems that although the Aryans retained the horse as their primary animal (the chariot of their fiery god Indra originally was pulled by horses), they gradually took over local 'elephant technology'.

Little wonder that Aryan kings and their successors also wished to ride the elephant, to incorporate the beast, both actual and mythological, into their expressions of power. The Dravidian peoples' use of the elephant as a war machine was adopted by the Aryans and by the more powerful and centralized kingdoms and republics over the course of the first millennium BC. Very early totemic beliefs combined with new political power structures; political patronage in turn ensured that the magnificence of the elephant became central to emerging religious belief systems.

As the Brahman and Hindu cosmologies evolved, the Aryan Indra, god of war, thunder and rain, came to be depicted riding an elephant named Airavata. Elephants were associated with the beginning of the world. The elephants Mahapadma – 'great forest' – and Saumanasa – 'keeper of *soma*, the sacred juice' – supported the whole world like two pillars. Elephants also represented fertility. Conventionally associated with rain-giving clouds as well as the stormy onset of musth, Indra mutated into Gajalakshmi – Lakshmi of the elephants. As Stephen Alter describes her statuesque presence at the temple of Kailash, Lakshmi 'emerges out of a lotus, containing the seeds of life within her, a vision of beauty and perfection, her breasts swollen, her gestures inviting elephants like clouds pouring water down on her, 'an active and essential part of creation'.[2]

Central to these religious developments was the creation of such traditional deities as the ever popular Ganesh or Ganesa.

So widespread is the worship and presence of Ganesh – from India to Indonesia, from Cambodia into China – that it's surprising to learn how late the figure emerged. Moreover, the evolution of Ganesh involves a bizarre transformation of early and rather malevolent deities known as *vinayakas* into their exact opposite. Vedic texts outlined several elephant-related deities, some of which involved epithets such as *Vighnesa* and *Vighnesara*, derived from *vighna*, an obstacle. These *vinayakas* were in places absorbed into a single, elephant-headed 'Lord of Obstacles' – who became, around the fifth century AD, Ganesh, the 'Remover of Obstacles'.

The development of the Ganesh figure was accompanied by a spreading taboo on the eating of elephant meat in northern India; both were tied directly to ecological realities. On the one hand, expanding agricultural societies were facing increased competition with elephants, and only an elephant-god could be called upon to defend them (hence Ganesh figures are usually accompanied by icons of sugarcane or a radish). At the same time, wild elephant populations were increasingly being diverted to military activities. Raman Sukumar therefore speculates that marginal societies found it economically more attractive to capture elephants for sale than to kill them for food or in defence of crops: the worship of Ganesh was first practised by the elite and only grudgingly accepted by the general populace. The 'religious' practice may, in short, have started as a power-ploy designed to make possible continued use of living elephants.[3]

Hence wherever elephants were tamed, kings and emperors, many of whom claimed divine rights, rode into ceremony and battle on their backs in gaudy pomp – a tradition that continued for another couple of millennia. In some early representations, it's hard to say whether the elephants are carrying military 'towers' or 'howdahs', throne-like seating arrangements, which became increasingly elaborate over time. A fine example is a painting, in gouache and gold on paper, from Bijapur in AD 1645, depicting the Sultan Muhammad Adil Shah riding his richly adorned elephant, with his prime minister, a former Ethiopian slave, behind him. The sultan carries the ankush, with its one straight and one hooked barb, both the instrument of training and direction and the symbol of political clout. (But it also depicts the chains around the elephant's ankles.) One such ankush is kept in the Victoria and Albert Museum in London, made in 1870 for the Maharaja of Jaipur, elaborately fashioned in gold and set with diamonds and enamel, its two hooks figured as snakes issuing from an elephant's mouth.

It was a sign of the shifts in power that in April 1876 the Prince of Wales would be seen climbing up an elephant's flank into a richly gilded howdah in order to proceed with his visit to imperial India. When the Prince was crowned Edward VII, Viceroy Lord Curzon organized the 1903 Delhi Durbar in celebration, consciously using a romanticized version of India's own elephant pageantry to emphasize British superiority. Curzon arrived impressively on a tusker adorned with a gold umbrella – which also, impressively, nearly panicked Lord Kitchener's thoroughbred. It was, famously, this pompous façade that George Orwell mocked in his brilliant essay 'Shooting an Elephant'.

Another ugly dimension of imperial elephant power was using them to hunt other animals. This practice has probably been in existence for as long as tamed elephants have: Plutarch, in his *Indica* (c. AD 100), wrote that to hunt mantichores (mythical) and tigers (real), 'men ride on elephants and shoot down at them'.[4] Better verified records are quite recent. The Mughal emperor Babur was depicted killing a rhinoceros from elephant-back in the early 1500s. His successor Akbar (1560–1605) organized huge shoots: one hunt, in 1567, was said to have lasted several days, 10,000 soldiers surrounding a zone 60 miles in diameter. Akbar ranged freely here, killing boars, tigers and lions with both spear and musket. The tiger hunt also carried over into British imperial times: Edward, Prince of Wales, witnessed a tiger attacking an elephant while on a hunt, during which he himself shot indiscriminately at bears and rhinos as well. Though the practice of hunting with the help of elephants is usually associated with India, it happened in Africa too.

To use an elephant for hunting, work or warfare obviously means having to catch it first. Capturing wild animals, each weighing several tons, is a dangerous and nasty business. Methods have changed little over the centuries. The earliest were probably derived from Palaeolithic methods of cornering mammoths: herd the target into a marshy area and harpoon or lasso it. This would be done during the rainy season: an elephant trapped in rising water by parties of harpoonists would have to swim in circles until exhausted enough to be tethered. Both Africans and Asians are known to have used pitfalls to capture elephants, but this method often fatally injured the animals. Methods of lassoing also varied. Lassoing by men on foot was obviously extremely hazardous; some people, like the *pannikians*, a Muslim sect in Sri Lanka, made it their speciality. Lassoing with the help of tame elephants – a process apparently alluded to by Aristotle in his *Historia animalum* and called *mela shikar* in India – was safer, but also could deal only with isolated individuals.

Much more efficient, and less lethal, was to harry a small herd into a staked enclosure, when selected animals could be drawn off and calmed by being tethered, starved and teamed up with already tame elephants (*koonkies* in India). Sometimes, females in oestrus were used to lure bulls into such traps: the

Always a brutal
business; bagging
a baby elephant
in Ceylon.

historian Arrian (AD 95–175) relates how females were at least
once used to tempt some bulls onto a bridge from which they
could not retreat. Even this process took its toll: animals would
naturally try to escape, counter-attack or try to help each other,
and it has been estimated that for every North African elephant
that reached the Roman arenas, nine died. It is always a stom-
ach-turning process: 'Babies are wrenched from their mothers,
bulls thrashed by the tame ones if they resist the nooses,
maddened members of the same herd butting each other in a
frantic bid to escape.'[5]

In Asia, the herding technique or *kheddah* became more refined – though it was far from always being successful. Hyder Ali, a ruler of Mysore, had tried to entrap elephants in India's Biligirirangan Hills, but had to leave a chastened monument to his failure: a stone marker on which he inscribed a curse on anyone else who tried to capture elephants. Into these same hills came, in 1873, one G. P. Sanderson, who persuaded British authorities to let him attempt a *kheddah*. An initial failure was followed by a success, which was then emulated throughout Asia. Sanderson went on to manage *kheddah*s in Burma, then returned to Mysore to be appointed 'Officer in Charge of Government Elephant Catching Establishment'. In fact, similar methods had been refined by Portuguese and Dutch colonials, too: figures from just one area of Sri Lanka record, amongst

Four elephants pulling a carriage in India, c. 1922.

INDIA – ELEPHANT FOUR-IN-HAND,   71-15

many, 96 elephants captured in a single Dutch *kraal* in 1666, 270 in 1681, 160 in 1690 and 400 in an English capture in 1797. Hundreds of elephants must have been exported as a result of these operations. The last Sri Lanka *kheddah* occurred in 1950; there, as in India, it has been superseded by gentler, chemical-tranquilizer forms of capture.

The taming of a young elephant, once also cruel and injurious, can take a matter of mere weeks if done with sensitivity. Further education has also been refined, though modern methods are only somewhat less soul-destroying than in the past. It took considerable training to override the elephant's fear of so primordial an enemy as a tiger or lion: from the era when sabre-toothed tigers predated upon mammoth calves, to modern Botswana, where one pride of lions has specialized in taking down even mature elephants, the big cats have always been the elephant's main predator – man excepted, of course. Paradoxically, training almost always depends on relationships of extraordinary closeness between elephant and handler – *mahout* in India, *oozie* in Burma – and a judicious mixture of rewards with food and goading some 85 known nerve centres with the ankush; eventually, most commands can be transmitted verbally or by the subtlest of movements of the rider's body on the elephant's shoulders.

Not that this was always effective under battle conditions. Everybody knows the story of Hannibal and his war elephants, but in fact he was one of the least successful and significant of elephant generals. The use of elephants in battle preceded him by at least a thousand years, mainly in India and China.

Pitiless and powerful are the elephants as a sword . . .
They do not give up their lives easily; elephants have magnificent bodies. Man or horse will die from an

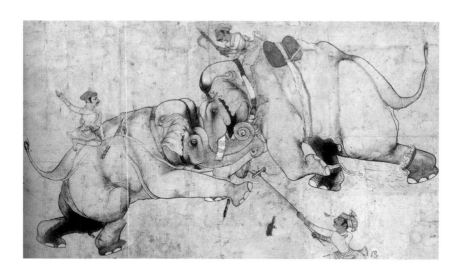

Elephants have been used in sport from the Roman gladiatorial contest to modern polo. Two fighting elephants, Kotah, Rajasthan, India, c. 1720.

ax-blow, but an elephant may survive a hundred ax-blows in battle. A warrior who abandons an elephant in battle treads the path to hell which lies in wait for the murderer of a Brahman . . . Where there are elephants, there is victory.[6]

So raves one slightly unrealistic early Indian account from the *Vedas*, which outlined the basic military unit or *patti* as consisting of one elephant, a chariot, three horses and five infantrymen; a typical massed formation might consist of 45 *pattis*. The elephants would lead the charge, throwing the enemy into confusion; each elephant, it was said, was worth 6,000 horses.

It was only with the advent of Western encounters with Asian war elephants, however, that any great detail was documented. It really began with eyewitness accounts of Alexander the Great (336–323 BC) and his confrontation with Porus's Asian elephant corps in the battle of the Hydaspes. Alexander had briefly encountered elephants at Gaugamela (331 BC); now, five years on, he even had 100 of his own, though they were not yet battle-trained. As it happened, even Porus's 200 elephants would not save him: Alexander's troops outflanked them, isolated them, slashed their trunks, targeted their mahouts, and drove them onto their own troops 'like ships backing'. Porus himself, it was said, started to slide from his elephant's back; the mahout ordered the elephant to kneel, whereupon so did all the others, as they had been trained, and so were captured. The elephant was even said to have tried to draw the spears from the king's body, and to defend him against those who tried to strip his armour.

Despite the elephants' limited effectiveness, the squabbling successor warlords who carved Alexander's ramshackle empire up between them – notably the Seleucids and the Ptolemies – continued to use elephants in battle. Perdiccas, the nominal regent, used elephants to execute some of his opponents by crushing their heads underfoot. He also attacked Ptolemy on the Nile, using elephants to tear down palisades, and even trying to use a row of them as a breakwater on the river: they were washed away, however, and many were eaten by crocodiles.

Inevitably, various generals began to develop anti-elephant technology; when Cassander besieged Polyperchon in Megalopolis, a kind of primitive minefield was laid using nail-studded frames to puncture the elephants' feet, so immobilizing them and making them more vulnerable to archers. Ptolemy did something similar at Gaza, Egypt, when attacked in 312 BC. The writer Diodorus noted of the elephants that 'on smooth and yielding ground they display an irresistible strength in a direct attack, but on rough and difficult ground their might is useless because of the tenderness of their feet.' Hence, though elephants continued to play a part in various struggles, they were seldom decisive, and were used as much to overawe as actually to attack. This seems to have been the gambit of the famous Pyrrhus, king of Epirus, when he introduced elephants to Italy, as much later immortalized in verse by Macaulay:

> The Greek shall come against thee,
>   The conqueror of the east;
> Beside him stalks to battle
>   The huge earth-shaking beast,
> The beast on whom the castle
>   With all its guards doth stand,
> The beast who hath between his eyes
>   The serpent for a hand.

Pyrrhus performed perhaps the longest transport of elephants by sea to date, when in 281 BC he crossed the Adriatic to Tarentum with twenty animals. Using them, he turned the tide of battle against the inexperienced Romans at Heraclea, and again at Apulia in 279 BC. In a final battle at Beneventum, however, his defeat was said to have been precipitated by a lost or injured elephant calf driving its mother mad with concern. Having been turfed out of Italy, Pyrrhus continued to use elephants in various Greek and Spartan adventures, including the siege of Argos. By this time, the use of elephant-back towers housing armoured bowmen seems to have been perfected; in this case, however, the city's gates were too low to admit them, and they had to be dismantled and reassembled inside. The delay was Pyrrhus' undoing; stunned by a rooftile, he was decapitated on the spot. Where his body was burned – said the traveller Pausanias 400 years later – a tomb was erected bearing relief-carvings of elephants.

Antiochus was another proponent of war elephants. In 275 BC he shocked the unsuspecting Gauls into undignified retreat, but rebuked his troops: 'Shame, my men, whose salvation came through these sixteen beasts. If the novelty of their appearance had not struck the enemy with panic, where should we have been?' When he invaded Syria almost half a century later, he found his elephants opposed by others. Polybius wrote of the battle at Raphia:

> Only some few of Ptolemy's elephants came to close quarters with their opponents, and the men in the towers on the back of these beasts made a gallant fight of it, lunging with their pikes (*sarissas*) at close quarters and striking each other, while the elephants themselves fought still more brilliantly, using all their strength in the encounter and pushing against each other, forehead to forehead . . . With their tusks firmly interlocked and entangled they push against each other with all their might, each trying to force the other to give ground, until the one who proves the strongest pushes aside the other's trunk, and then, when he has once made him turn, he gores him . . . [7]

The result was a truce; as would be learned repeatedly, elephants seldom decided a battle. Antiochus also used elephants in an ongoing quarrel with the Jews; in the same sphere of operations, as recorded in 1 Maccabees, Judas advanced on the Syrians' royal pavilion, which was defended by elephants:

> The elephants were roused for battle with the juice of grapes and mulberries. The great beasts were distributed amongst the phalanxes; behind each were stationed a

thousand men, equipped with coats of chain-mail and bronze helmets. Five hundred picked horsemen were also assigned to each animal. These had been stationed beforehand where the beast was; and wherever it went, they went with it, never leaving it. Each animal had a strong wooden turret fastened on its back with a special harness, by way of protection, and carried four fighting men as well as an Indian driver.

Judas's brother Eleazar, mistaking a richly decorated elephant for the royal one, ran in beneath it and stabbed it through the belly, but the animal collapsed on top of him and crushed him.

Once Pyrrhus had retreated from Italy, the main regional conflicts were Roman–Carthaginian. Carthaginian forces from North Africa had faced Pyrrhus' elephants in Sicily, and followed the fashion. Perhaps for the first time, North African elephants were now captured and trained like their Asian counterparts (though they had long been hunted). Contrary to popular belief, they are no less (or more) tractable. A Spartan mercenary,

Henri-Paul Motte, c. 1890, depicted the Carthaginians taking elephants into the battle of Zama in 202 BC.

H. Leutemann dramatically rendered Hannibal's passage through the Alps in a coloured wood engraving, c. 1865. The truth is, of course, that no elephants fell.

Xanthippos, successfully used elephants to hasten the retreat of a Roman invasion; the Carthaginian generals Hasdrubal, Hanno and Hamilcar all used elephants, though with mixed results. Hasdrubal lost a small herd to the Roman Metellus, who shipped his elephant captives back across the Straits of Messina on earth-covered rafts. But as H. H. Scullard writes in his classic study of this period, *The Elephant in the Greek and*

J. H. Williams escapes from Burma with his elephants in 1943, an illustration from his book *Elephant Bill* (1954).

Roman World, 'One thing is clear: the Romans apparently decided that they provided too double-edged a weapon for adoption in their own army.'[8]

Taking over the Carthaginians' invasion of Spain in 221 BC, the famous Hannibal pushed across the Rhone with 37 elephants, eluded the countering force of Scipio, and embarked on his renowned Alpine trek over the 8,143-foot (2,450-m) Clapier Pass. Despite being held up for three snowy days by a landslide, he crossed into northern Italy without losing a single elephant. When he joined battle on the River Trebia, however, only seven of the elephants involved survived. Hannibal fought on, losing more elephants to cold in the Appenines, but became increasingly besieged in the south of Italy. In a vain effort to relieve him, Hasdrubal used elephants but, at a battle in the valley of the Metaurus, they panicked and caused equal havoc to both sides. The last poor survivors of Hannibal's Alpine crossing had to be killed by their own mahouts driving chisels into their necks with mallets. When the Third Punic War began fifty years later, the Carthaginians had no elephants at all.

Hannibal's trek nevertheless remains the classic story of war-elephant adventure. When in 1943 J. H. Williams – the famous 'Elephant Bill', colonial Burma's number one elephant organizer – had to make an epic escape into India with women, children and elephants ahead of the Japanese invasion, he explicitly compared his trek across precipitous mountains to Hannibal's. In September 1979 some intrepid circus-elephant owners and their animals even repeated Hannibal's feat, finding the descent of the Col de Clapier the most hazardous section.

The Romans, for their part, liked to have some elephants around, but seldom used them in battle. Julius Caesar was rumoured to have brought an elephant into Britain (some thought the word *caesar* was in fact Moorish for elephant), but it seems unlikely. Certainly, however, he was escorted back into Rome with a triumphal retinue of 40 elephants; he, like many of

Elephants on coins were used by Julius Caesar and many other Romans to convey power; this shows Quintus Caecilius Metellus Pius, c. 81 BC.

his predecessors, had coins minted using elephant motifs as symbols of imperial power. The main demonstration of Roman power, however, would be using the hapless elephants in various, usually bloody, arena entertainments, rather than in battle. As Livy succinctly put it: 'elephantomachae nomen tantum sine usu fuerunt' ('the elephant-fighters were a mere name without practical effect').

The disappearance of elephants from the post-Roman European consciousness, as well as the lingering allure of elephants as war-machines, is much later reflected in J.R.R Tolkien's fantasy *The Lord of the Rings*. Sam the hobbit recites a rather silly poem about 'oliphaunts', which have in his society become entirely mythical. Tolkien doubtless derived the name from the Middle English *olifant* or *olifaunt*, which could mean both elephant and a horn made from elephant ivory – the most famous example of which was used (too late to save the battle) at Roncesvalles in the Pyrenees in AD 778 by the eponymous hero of the *Chanson de Roland*. In Tolkien's epic, the adventuring hobbits do later encounter actual oliphaunts and mammoth-like *mûmakil* bearing, like their real-life originals, siege-towers and warriors, with 'great legs like trees, enormous sail-like ears spread out, long snout upraised like a huge serpent about to strike'.[9] Tolkien, again echoing the real world, strikes an elegiac note in the final book of his trilogy about the disappearance from 'Middle Earth' of these vast monsters.

Elephants continued to be used as a vital component of battle formations in the East, however. The most prominent king of the second great Persian or Sassanid empire, Shapur II (ruled AD 309–79), used elephants both against the Romans and to crush a Christian rebellion at the city of Susa, which he razed to the ground. When Timur and his Mongols attacked Delhi in 1398, he faced not only 30,000 Indian foot-soldiers, but a fearsome phalanx of war elephants; he scotched them, however, by loading buffaloes and camels with hay and setting them alight amongst the elephants, which understandably panicked. Babur (1483–1530), founder of India's Mughal dynasty, used elephants alongside his cavalry, and left a remarkable autobiography in Turkish, the *Baburnama*, which included a knowledgeable chapter on Asian elephants. Babur's grandson Akbar (ruled 1560–1605) became more famous still for his elephant-taming skills, claiming to have a God-given gift for handling even bulls in musth 'which had killed their drivers and were man-slayers'. The *Akbarnama*, written by Abu Fazl, trumpeted his praises:

> When India was made illustrious by his blessed advent [Akbar] gave special attention to elephants, which are wonderful animals in both form and in ways. If in respect of size I liken them to a mountain . . . I do not succeed in my attempt . . . If I compare them in foresight, intelligence and sagacity to the horse the real thing is not said.[10]

Akbar inherited, captured and stabled thousands of elephants in his time. He left also some remarkable painted miniatures of his elephants in both war and entertainment; he was particularly celebrated for subduing the fortress of Muslim rival Uday-Singh, Chitor, in 1567 and two years later that of Ranthambhor, using elephants on both occasions. They were his primary symbol of power, as Abu Fazl recorded:

> The biggest and strongest of the imperial elephants bears the title of 'Elephant General'. When he appears at court adorned with costly caparisons, he is awaited in great pageantry by a line of elephants and honoured with flutes, trumpets and cymbals, and a great show of flags . . . [11]

An elephant accompanies warriors to battle in the Belur-Halebid stone relief from the Hoysala Empire of southern India, *c.* 1200.

War elephant on a stone relief at Ankhor Thom, Cambodia.

Elephants thereafter seemed more prominent amongst the Mughals as ceremonial accoutrements than as war machines, right up to the advent of British rule. Further south, in Ceylon or Sri Lanka, which had supplied elephants to the northern kings since Alexander's time, armies also used war elephants at times. The Ceylonese royal chronicle tells the story of one Kandula, a war elephant instrumental in fending off attacks from a South Indian Tamil invader, Elala. Kandula, it is said, head-charged the gates of Elala's fortress. Temporarily repelled by red-hot iron balls and boiling pitch, Kandula went off to a pool to cool his wounds before returning to the attack with renewed energy, succeeding at last in staving in the doors.

Further east still, Burma (now Myanmar) and neighbouring countries had a highly developed elephant culture, including war elephants. Carvings on the walls of Cambodia's Angkor Wat, dating from the early twelfth century, show elephants in battle. In 1283 a Chinese mounted army under Kublai Khan annihilated the King of Burma's forces, including routing and capturing his hundreds of war elephants. The traveller Marco Polo, who left a vivid account of this battle, also noted how prominent elephants were in the Chinese Middle Kingdom's ceremonials, even though the elephant as wild resident had long disappeared from almost the whole of China. Polo described Khan's massive command post:

> Kublai sat in a large wooden structure, carried by four elephants whose bodies were covered with armour of thick leather hardened in the fire; the armour, however, was covered with cloths interwoven with gold. Many crossbowmen and archers were posted in the structure and above fluttered the imperial standard . . . [12]

South-east Asian leaders persisted in using elephants: as late as the mid-nineteenth century the king of Siam possessed a force of 400 battle-trained elephants, clad in hardened leather and iron-plate armour and carrying small howitzers on their backs. Thereafter, however, the use of elephants as participants in battle declined everywhere, increasingly sidelined by the advent of firearms and mechanized transport. Nowhere was

Elephants have from time to time been recorded pulling ploughs: this is perhaps the earliest, a medieval illustration for an edition of Pliny's *Historia naturalis*.

this more obvious, perhaps, than in the war of 1824, when Burma, embroiled in French–British conflicts, attacked Assam; its elephants proved no match for British guns. Nevertheless, before and after the 1886 incorporation of all Burma into the British Empire, elephants were used by all sides to haul guns, build roads and bridges, and transport men over terrain where horses and vehicles were useless. The British Army in India used elephants similarly, as well as to overawe minor tribes, notably deploying an Anglo-Gurkha elephant squadron on the border with Afghanistan.

As and when conflicts developed, working elephants were regularly dragooned back into war service. J. H. Williams, as he recounts in his classic book *Elephant Bill*, found himself using his logging elephants to assist the Allied war effort against the Japanese invaders, who themselves used an elephant corps to force their way through the Malaysian jungles. They captured each others' animals, and many died or were wounded in firefights. These uses continued into the modern era: the

Vietnamese king used elephants for jungle transport during Vietnam's earliest struggles for independence, and in the 1960s elephants were instrumental in opening up the 'Ho Chi Minh' trail so vital to Vietnam's resistance to American attack. Cambodian troops also used elephants against the Viet Cong.

Odd individuals also found themselves absorbed into theatres of war elsewhere. During the First World War the German army commandeered an Indian elephant from the Hagenbeck Zoo in Hamburg. 'Jenny' was deployed to the French front, where she moved tons of *matériel* and building timbers and helped plough fields. Another of Hagenbeck's elephants was deployed to Belgium, and was photographed moving logs in 1915 for *T. P.'s Journal of Great Deeds*, under the alarming headline 'The Forests of France and Belgium: How War is Destroying Them'. Another Asian elephant, 'Unofficially Attached to Mr Lloyd George's Department', was photographed in Sheffield's grimy railyards, hauling some daunting-looking piece of machinery.

Elephant working with logs in India, date unknown.

This kind of work is, in fact, how most living elephants have been used: to move heavy objects, mostly logs, and to open up roads in marshy or mountainous conditions. Early rulers used elephants to haul materials for their extravagant building projects. Timur, for instance, is said to have employed a permanent contingent of 95 elephants when building the mosque at Samarkand. They are best known, however, for their involvement in the destruction of their own habitat under British rule in South-east Asia. There, throughout Siam, Burma and Sumatra, imperialist, and then multinational, logging operations have been responsible for the denudation of hundreds of thousands of square miles of hardwood forest. Some 250 million hectares of tropical hardwood forest extant in 1900 have now been reduced to less than 60 million hectares, and this figure is falling. Much could not have been achieved without the help of elephants. J. H. Williams recorded that one of his logging elephants, Bandoola, in one season 'extracted three hundred tons of teak an average distance of two miles from stump to floating-stream'.[13] Hundreds of thousands of wild elephants inhabited the Asian forests at the beginning of the twentieth century; today there are less than 35,000. At the same time, compared to the 100,000 tamed elephants of Thailand in 1900, only some 4,000 still work, though new opportunities open up from time to time. An additional pressure is that very little captive breeding occurs, so that replacements still have to be obtained from the wild.

Whatever the hardships of rolling and dragging massive logs – some weighing up to 4 tons – the logging elephants' lives are not wholly deprived. At best, they are carefully tended, work limited hours, get a supplementary diet of rice balls mixed with fat, sugar-cane and bread, spend hours bonding with their mahouts in extended and necessary bathing times, and often are permitted some time wandering, albeit hobbled, in their natural forest habitat. The best tended certainly have a better time of it than their counterparts in Western zoos, and perhaps even in the various elephant orphanages and reserves that have tried to absorb the growing population of elephants discarded by the logging industry. Raman Sukumar found three working elephants that had lived beyond 75 years, 'unthinkable in a zoo'. The freer communities in Tamilnadu and Myanmar also show higher breeding rates and slower demographic decline than anywhere else in captive populations. (In Western zoos, by contrast, elephant numbers – unless replaced from outside – decline at a rate of 8 per cent, since they scarcely breed; and fewer than 30 per cent live beyond 40 years of age.)

In perhaps the most recently celebrated example of helpful elephants, Sri Lankan and Thai animals helped in rescue efforts when the 2004 tsunami hit their coastlines. According to mahouts at Khao Lak beach resort in Thailand, the elephants 'cried' quite uncharacteristically before the tsunami struck, then ran for the hills, pausing only to pluck up some fleeing tourists. Much scepticism has been expressed about the more heroic stories of elephants selflessly snatching people to safety. Scientists noted that radio-collared elephants, close to shore in Sri Lanka's Yala National Park, had exhibited no tendency to move inland when the tsunami arrived. But there seems little reason to doubt that many of the elephants, along with birds and dogs, displayed some sense of impending change. At any rate, elephants proved useful in various places to help remove debris and search for bodies before mechanized lifting gear arrived.

In 2003 Sukumar estimated that 14,500–15,000 elephants (about a third of the Asian total) lived in various forms of captivity in their range states, broken down roughly as follows:

Myanmar 5,000, Thailand 4,000, India 3,500, Laos 1,350, Cambodia 300, Sumatra 362, Sri Lanka 227, Nepal 171, and Vietnam 165. Everywhere, as Mark Shand has pointed out in *Queen of the Elephants*, his lively account of an elephant trek across India with woman mahout-*extraordinaire* Parbati Bihar, the elephants (and the authorities) are caught in a double bind. As demand for captive elephants falls, wild populations increase, but habitat is still being denuded, so that conflict with humans increases. There are simply fewer and fewer places for elephants, wild or captive, to go. Outside Asia, perhaps a thousand Asian elephants subsist in zoo or circus situations (one organization estimates that there are 90 elephants in German circuses alone).

If you google 'elephants in circuses' you will be faced with a welter of sites attacking the abuse of elephants – and scarcely a site defending their use. There is arguably a narrow line between adorning elephants for controlled parades in religious worship and adorning elephants for controlled entertainment in a circus ring, or being used for a game of 'elephant polo'. In the West, however, compelling elephants into tortuous positions – balancing on their heads, on bicycles, or on tiny stools – has reached its peak of exploitation. It began, no doubt, with the Roman games, where elephants were goaded into fighting gladiators, lions or each other for the bloodthirsty hordes in the Circus Maximus. But even then, if Pliny's first-century BC account is to be believed, one courageous elephant's bearing had the crowd on its feet in sympathetic uproar. Pliny also recorded that elephants were already being taught to dance, balance on tightropes and fling pebbles.

It was the Americans who were primarily responsible for the razzmatazz of the modern circus act – beginning symbolically with P. T. Barnum's notorious 'theft' of the London elephant 'Jumbo' in 1882 (poor Jumbo didn't last long, dying at 25 in a train accident). Circuses proliferated into the twentieth century, and you can now view online any number of sickening video clips of circus handlers thrashing performing elephants into compliance with a bullhook (ankush), electrified cattle prod or simple iron bar. Celebrated cases recently have been the 'escape' of Janet, a terrified circus elephant who 'ran amok' in Palm Bay, Florida, in 1992, with a mother and five children on her back – a traffic officer had to kill her, taking 34 inexperienced shots to do it – and that of the Ringling Brothers circus group being brought to court in 2006 for elephant abuse. Some 40 Americans, mostly handlers, have been killed by captive, ostensibly tamed elephants (not to mention many Asian mahouts).[14] The most absurd example recently was of one Friedrich Riesveld in Paderborn, Germany, who fed his constipated elephant Stefan 22 doses of animal laxative, berries and bushels of

Poster for the Ringling Brothers' elephant brass band, c. 1899.

141

prunes, before resorting to an olive oil enema – which abruptly worked, burying and suffocating the surprised keeper under 200 pounds of dung.

The litany of such examples might testify to the energy of the animal rights lobbyists more than to the actual scale of the problem. One researcher, while noting that the traditional practice of picketing or chaining elephants resulted in higher incidences of stereotypic weaving or rocking behaviour and more erratic performance, still concluded that elephants were as well treated as other species in stables or kennels.[15] This ignores, of course, the massive differences between an elephant and a horse or dog. There seems little reason to doubt that circus acts serve next to no educational purpose, and that the lives of travelling elephants, obliged to perform physically unnatural and demeaning tricks, caged or chained when at rest, and boxed in for many hours while on the road, live a pretty miserable life compared to those in the wild.

At least some circuses have tried to develop more humane methods of gaining compliance from their elephants. Ralph Helfer, for one, became a well-known trainer to animals in an astonishing 5,000 Hollywood movies. He used gentleness and reward as his primary tools, even with lions and elephants. Helfer's book *Modoc* (and the spin-off film, starring Kevin Costner) is not exactly 'the true story of the greatest elephant that ever lived' that its subtitle proclaims. One acute reviewer noted that Ringling Brothers – for whom Helfer worked for a time – had had at least three elephants named Modoc, none of whom had lived very long. Still, as a novel, *Modoc* is a tear-jerker that has stimulated a number of readers to make the journey to the real elephant sanctuary at Hohenwald, Tennessee, in which Helfer has also been involved. Among others, Helfer purchased and took to Hohenwald an abused and dangerous

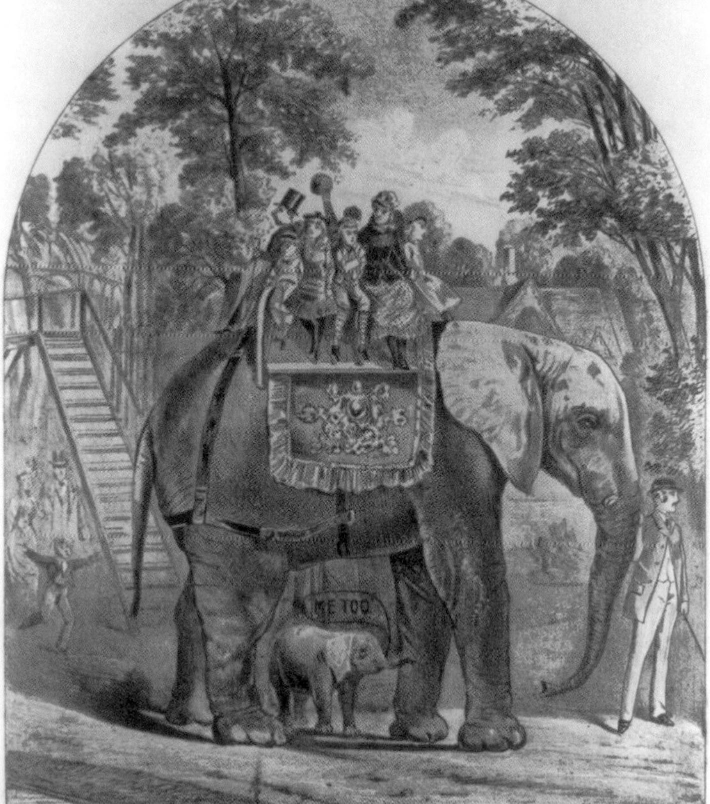

elephant named Misty, whose story recalls that of 'Modoc' in that she had been passed from circus to circus before finding sanctuary at Hohenwald. Hohenwald, with its 2,700 acres, is one of the few places in America where discarded elephants from circuses and zoos can go and experience something resembling a free life.

A considerable number of elephant sanctuaries have sprung up, both in the West and in Asia, to take in the orphans and the retired of the shrinking numbers of both zoos and logging camps. Even here, it's difficult to avoid the sense that the elephants are being exploited for mere entertainment, whatever the arguments that educational and conservation purposes are being served, or that the elephants are helping pay for themselves. One example is the elephant xylophone band, concocted by Richard Lair and David Soldier at the Thai Elephant Conservation Centre – buy the CD! They claim the elephants choose the notes themselves. This is not, incidentally, so new; the great French essayist Montaigne, in *An Apologie of Raymond Sebond*, reminds us that the historian Arrian (here in a 1603 translation)

> protesteth to have seene an Elephant, who on every thigh having a cimball hanging, and one fastened to his truncke, at the sound of which, all other Elephants danced in a round, now rising aloft, then lowing full at certaine cadences, even as the instrument directed them, and was much delighted at the harmony . . . Some [elephants] have beene noted to konne and practice their lessons, using much study and care, as being loath to be chidden and beaten of their masters.

There's the rub, of course.

Another, avowedly gentler example is the Asian Elephant Art and Conservation Project in Thailand, which pays for tending its elephant orphans partly with funds raised from sales of the elephants' own paintings – an idea that, as their mission statement proclaims, certainly 'pushes the boundaries of art as charity, while questioning our notions of artist and intent'! For $400, you can buy a non-toxic painting – and the elephants do seem to develop individual styles.[16]

And then there are all the 'elephant-back safari' operations that have recently proliferated – what has been a commonplace in Asia for millennia is still more of a novelty in Africa. I found communing with elephants through eye and fingertip contact, in both Zimbabwe and South Africa, a soulful and awe-inspiring experience, but riding on top of one taught me nothing further, and seemed to me just another extension of our smug notions of superiority and control. This is so even if it provides actress Cameron Diaz with a spectacular opportunity to promote conservation issues, and reaches its nadir when elephants are used as backdrop and carriage for bikini-clad models for *Sports Illustrated*. Many are now arguing against elephant-back safaris. Capture methods have been widely challenged, and Rick Allen, head of the NSPCA's wildlife unit in South Africa, has said: 'Any claim that this type of capture and training for commercial use is in the interests of conservation is stretching the point to fairytale proportions.'[17] Late 2007 saw a landmark legal decision when a South African court found in favour of an SPCA suit to prevent a tourist park acquiring and training elephants specifically for riding 'safaris'; and in February 2008 South African protocols were legislated banning the capture of any elephants for safari or circus use. (It's not even terribly comfortable, as raconteur Peter Ustinov once quipped: 'There's more room on a Vespa than there is on the back of an elephant.')

From a Japanese Menagerie, *Elephant*, 1871–89, signed *Kyosai ga*, seal: *Issho keiko* ('All my life just practising').

These captive-elephant operations are sometimes not far removed from those rather older sites of animal captivity: zoos. Zoos of one description or another have existed for thousands of years, too, and elephants are naturally quite a prize. Early

Most elephant paintings are 'abstract'; Tukta, a 13-year-old female, produces more naturalistic images.

Egyptian pharoahs may have included elephants in collections of wild animals. Around 1000 BC the legendary Solomon – apart from his extravagant throne made of ivory – may have possessed elephants. Certainly Ashurbanipal of Assyria, ruling around 630 BC, had more than one elephant in one of the earliest known 'zoological gardens'. Alexander the Great sent elephants back to Macedonia for his tutor Aristotle to study, and a number of Greek city-states had animal collections that might have included elephants. Around 280 BC Ptolemy II built up a zoological collection in Alexandria that was the largest the world had known; ceremonial parades took a whole day to pass by, and typically included 96 elephants. The early Chinese also established zoos: Wen Wang, ruling around 1000 BC, established a 1,500-hectare so-called Garden of Intelligence or Lu-Ying. Though elephants probably were always centres of attraction, it is only with Kublai Khan, as witnessed by Marco Polo, that we have unambiguous evidence for their presence in Chinese zoos.

As we've seen, in the West elephants receded into almost mythical realms, until real elephants began again to be imported, at first as gifts to rulers for private menageries. Charlemagne's elephant, given to him by Harun al Rashid, was perhaps the most celebrated, followed by those acquired by Frederick II, Lorenzo the Magnificent and Louis XIV, among others. By the late sixteenth century, a number of elephants were present in captivity in Europe and England, occupying 'an ambiguous status between fighting animal and grand curio'.[18]

The transition from royal menagerie or 'seraglio' and travelling fair to modern zoo has been traced in detail by Eric Baratay and Elisabeth Hardouin-Fugier in their excellent book, *Zoo*. Suffice it to say here that only in the nineteenth century did the zoo acquire its modern form – that is, as a publicly funded insti-

At least some elephants reached Japan: 'Big imported elephant' is a woodcut on paper by Yoshitoyo Utagawa (1830–1866).

Poor substitute for a river: an elephant in an American zoo, c. 1926.

tution aimed not merely at entertaining the public, but also with species-preservation and research roles. As zoos mushroomed, along with both new urban wealth and scientific curiosity, so did captive elephant numbers. Members of the International Species Information Systems listed 100 bulls and 378 cows worldwide in 2002; one website lists 296 Asian elephants in European zoos in 2006, and 144 in North America.[19] (No one is sure how many illegal animals are being held.) Numbers of elephants in public institutions have thus remained fairly stable over the last few years.

Justifications for keeping them, however, are being increasingly challenged. The educational argument was put succinctly by Peper Long of the National Zoo in Washington, DC: 'For the 1.8 million people who come to the National Zoo each year, there is no replacement for a living elephant.'[20] Many assert that film footage is now so wonderful that keeping elephants in captivity is scarcely warranted. Today, although knowledge of elephant physiology and behaviour is better (indeed, often available only through zoo animals) and the architectures of captivity have gradually improved, the situation for the elephants themselves is not pretty. One zoo director, quoted recently in *Time* magazine, has 'come to the conclusion after many years that it is simply not possible for zoos to meet the needs of elephants'.[21]

Another commonly expressed justification – that captive-breeding programmes are going to be essential to replenishing elephant stock threatened in the wild – remains rather dubious. They are not yet self-replenishing. Replacement elephants have always had to be captured from the wild: Carl Hagenbeck, one of the most famous performing-elephant entrepreneurs, found himself 'too often obliged to kill' female elephants trying to save their babies from capture[22] – and this remains largely true. Though today more babies are being born in captivity, most are stillborn or die before they are six years old. There are no captive families of viable size; artificial insemination is possible but still difficult; shipping males to females elsewhere is prohibitively expensive and stressful. Hence one researcher titled his article on the subject: 'Asian Elephants in Zoos Face Global Extinction: Should Zoos Accept the Inevitable?'[23] Nevertheless, the controversy-dogged Ringling Brothers circus can carry on its website a notice that is at once defensive and boastful:

Japanese Menagerie: Elephants at Play, Fourth Month, a woodblock print of 1863.

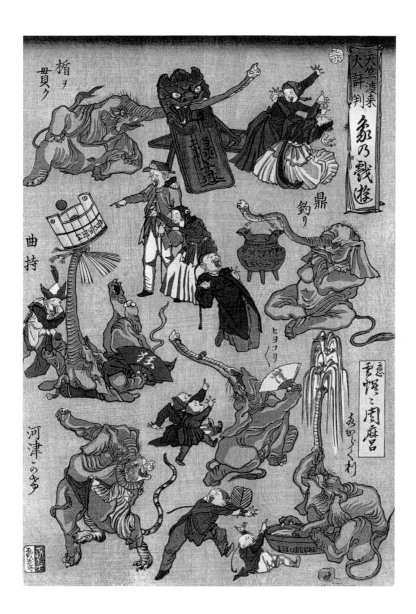

Ringling Bros. and Barnum & Bailey is the finest circus in the world. It is important to note that Ringling Bros. maintains the largest breeding herd of Asian elephants in the world outside of Tampa (Fla.). Without some of the work that Ringling Bros. has done with the Asian elephant, right or wrong, the Asian elephant might not be here 50 or 100 years from now. That's just a fact.[24]

What 'might be' is not yet a 'fact', and there is certainly argument about whether such a programme is 'right or wrong'; this ad neatly sums up the dilemmas and mixed feelings affecting elephant domestication. But here we are encroaching on the topic of our final chapter: the conservation of the elephant in today's increasingly crowded world.

5 Conservation

The present-day situation for the wild elephant – like almost any other 'charismatic megafauna' that you could name – is generally dire. The recent efforts to reverse the trend by zoos and national parks, international conservation agencies and government legislation, are rearguard actions; they are all but overwhelmed by human population growth, which now additionally unfolds against the backdrop of deleterious climate change. The reasons are simple: people have killed too many elephants for their ivory; and too many people have robbed the elephants of their historical habitat. As we have seen, elephants have always been hunted and used by humans in a multiplicity of ways, some uncaring, some worshipful. But the number of elephants captured alive for warfare, for circuses and zoos, for food, logging and religion, while widespread, pales into insignificance against the numbers killed for their tusks.

Human lust for ivory is the elephants' curse; trade in ivory is almost as old as trade itself. Probably killing for ivory grew out of utilizing naturally deceased animals; ancient Siberians used mammoth tusks to prop up their tents before they discovered they could sell them to the Chinese. Eventually, this trade flourished: between 1825 and 1914 an estimated 2,000 tons exited the port of Yakutsk alone. Although the Soviet Union gradually clamped down on it, the mammoth 'fossil ivory' business remains a complicating mask for trade in elephant ivory to this day.

Various peoples centralized elephant ivory trading over the millennia: the Harappans, the Phoenicians, the Romans and the Parthians. Each in turn controlled the main routes into Europe and the Middle East, or along the Silk Road into China. Most likely North African elephants were driven into extinction by ivory hunters by the end of the Roman empire; Pliny complained of a shortage of ivory in AD 77. In the rest of Africa, outside traders turned light and natural local use into a massacre. Arab slavers, Portuguese merchantmen and Swahili middlemen drove the trade out of East Africa – mostly to India, oddly, African ivory being considered finer than Asian. Asian ivory was often burned in religious ceremonies, too, so European carvers supplemented walrus and hippopotamus ivory with elephant ivory from Egypt, Ethiopia and later West Africa.

In Europe's Middle Ages ivory was reputed to have come from the mythical realms of the Queen of Sheba; another myth was that it was the horn of the unicorn, the symbol of virginity. Hence it was particularly used for religious icons devoted to the Virgin Mary. Crucifixes, diptychs and triptychs depicting biblical scenes, reliquaries, crosiers, rosary beads and other religious objects and statues abounded. (Dante, oddly, wrote of ivory as symbolizing falsehood.) The fourteenth century saw expanded use of ivory in a wealth of secular objects: cobblers' measures, spindles, hourglasses, belt-buckles, plaques depicting newly rediscovered classical scenes, casket lids and mirror-cases, covers for writing-tablets, dagger-handles, falcons' hood-rests, saddle cantles and dice-boxes, harp frames and spoons and powder-flasks, even shoes and ice-skates.[1] Many examples have to count amongst the finest examples of carving anywhere in history.

Between 1500 and 1700, in one estimation, an average of more than 100 tons of ivory left Africa annually; in the later years, India alone imported over 250 tons a year, a lot of it finding its way back from Mughal workshops, fetchingly carved, to the West. Fifteenth-century Benin was transformed by Portuguese entrepreneurs, who fostered a remarkable tradition of local carving, particularly associated with royalty, as well as expanding demand from enriched Europe for combs, knife-handles, chessmen, inlays for furniture and a hundred other luxuries.[2] The Japanese developed a unique tradition of ivory carvings in the form of tiny *netsuke* for attaching items to men's sashes. (These can be valuable: if you visit the Los Angeles Police Department website, you'll find in the Art Theft section the photo of a stolen beautiful nineteenth-century *netsuke* depicting Chinese children playing with an elephant.) Whole communities from Scotland and Dieppe to Samarkand and Hong Kong, Kyoto and Osaka, would eventually be founded on ivory-carving specialities.

Slaughter by the thousand: an East African ivory warehouse in the early 20th century.

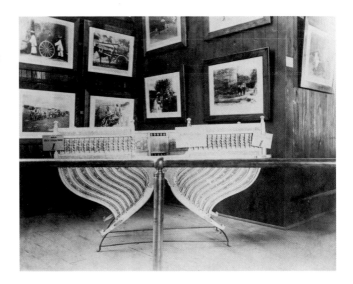

An uncomfortable-looking ivory 'saddle', from the World's Columbian Exposition, Chicago, 1893.

It was eighteenth- and nineteenth-century increases in demand from America, Europe and China that had the most dramatic effect. European colonization, coupled with the progression of firearms from muzzle-loading muskets to breech-loading rifles, made it possible to meet the fantastic demand for – amongst other things – piano keys and billiard-balls. American production of pianos rocketed from 9,000 in 1852 to 350,000 in 1910. All used porous, tactile ivory – a pound and a half in every keyboard. Between the same years, Britain alone imported around 500 tons of ivory annually, about half of the world's demand. This entailed the deaths of maybe 65,000 elephants every year. African middlemen, like the infamous Tippu Tip, flourished. Zanzibar was the main channel for thousands of tusks, brought in literally on the back of slaves, out to the East, where ivory in vast quantities was used for Indian marriage bangles and Chinese carvings and inks. The inherent violence of slaving and ivory extraction together had dramatic effects on both ecologies and societies inland of Africa's coasts, being implicated, to take just one example, in the rise of Shaka's Zulu state as early as the 1810s. When Henry Morton Stanley crossed the Congo towards his legendary rendezvous with David Livingstone, he made the following reckoning:

> Every pound weight [of ivory] has cost the life of a man, woman, or child; for every five pounds a hut has been burned; for every two tusks a village has been destroyed; every twenty tusks have been obtained at the price of a district with all its people, villages, and plantations.[3]

Aside from pure profit, the male ego was involved, too. The lure of the 'tusker' – immortalized in that ugliest of records,

African slaves were forced to carry ivory to the coasts, as depicted in Henry Rider Haggard's novel *Maiwa's Revenge* (1888).

Rowland Ward's compendium of trophy sizes – drew the early hunters: the bigger the tusks, the braver the man, was the message. In the course of a century, in short, elephant populations were decimated, to the point where hunters themselves began to warn of impending extinction in many regions. In 1881 that most archetypal of Great White Hunters, Frederick Courteney Selous, noted 'every year elephants were becoming scarcer and wilder south of the Zambezi, so that it had become almost impossible to make a living by hunting at all'.[4] In a curious, not entirely defensible way, hunters like Selous also prided themselves on providing 'specimens' for European museums. This almost accidental but educational aspect to their depredations was the precursor to more scientific investigation of the animals *in situ*. As an example of this shift, on 6 December 1905 the director of the Natural History Museum in Paris gathered a number of luminaries, including the composer Camille Saint-Saëns, to found the Society of the Friends of the Elephant – the first of many such. One Paul Hippeau enlivened proceedings with some doggerel, which sang in part:

> The elephant, it's a notorious fact,
> In Africa is disappearing.
> If we don't hasten to look at that,
> How can we remedy it?
> The elephant is a friend to man;
> More than the dog, it's constant.
> And now indeed our turn has come
> To be the friend to the elephant.[5]

Along with the demise of many other species as observed by more and more biological scientists, the plummeting number of elephants helped to stimulate the development of new conservationist approaches. In East and southern Africa in particular, it fed into the establishment of dedicated game reserves around the turn of the twentieth century, notably Kruger National Park in South Africa. Other countries were slower to legislate protected areas. In Kenya, Tsavo was proclaimed a reserve only in 1948 and Serengeti in 1951 (the same year, incidentally, as the first national parks were established in Britain). In Asia, too, reserves began to be designated: India's Kaziranga National Park in 1905 and Jim Corbett in 1936, for instance. Generally, progress was slow here, too: India's primary elephant park, Nagarahole, was proclaimed only in 1955. In Thailand, the first national park, Khao Yao, was set up in 1961. Laos is even further behind, establishing its National Biodiversity Conservation Areas (some 21 per cent of the country) as recently as 1993. This means that frameworks for protecting individual species such as elephant have for too long been of slender effect.

This explicitly conservationist development did not stop the ivory trade, but gave it a different spin. For poachers, concentrated populations of elephants in reserves became handy resources. Though global demand for ivory crashed after the First World War, and elephants began to make something of a recovery, the danger was not over. In the 1970s and '80s a wave of ivory poaching shattered the complacency of game reserves throughout Africa. Much of the demand came from China and from newly prosperous Japan, where ivory *hanko* (signature seals) were enjoying huge popularity (two million made in 1988 alone). Ivory prices soared from us$5.50 a kilogram in 1969 to $74 in 1978, to $300 in 1989. Demand by the rich at one end, local poverty at the other, and multiple opportunities for lucrative middlemen in between conspired to generate a murderous momentum. David Sheldrick in Kenya's Tsavo reserve, amongst other wardens, found himself engaged in – and often lost – protracted gun battles with raiders heavily armed with automatic weapons. By 1976 he figured he had lost half of Tsavo's elephants, adding to losses incurred in a particularly bad drought (6,000 died in 1969–70). Iain and Oria Douglas-Hamilton, who in the course of their pioneering studies in Manyara had developed closely personalized relationships with the elephants, were devastated in the mid-1980s to find their precious herds massively depleted. These experiences (recounted in their book *Among the Elephants*) were parallelled across the continent. (And the threat, albeit much reduced, continues: seven elephants were killed by ivory poachers in Tsavo during the month of June 2007.)

The governments of the range states were largely either too weak to act effectively or were actually complicit in the ivory trade. Moreover, Western agencies that wanted to help were at loggerheads over the scale of the problem and what to do about it. A dispute between Douglas-Hamilton and another Kenya-based conservationist, Ian Parker, focused the problems. One issue was knowing just how many animals there were. Parker estimated almost twice the number that Douglas-Hamilton did, underplayed the threat and argued for a continuation of the ivory trade under controlled conditions. Although it turned out that Parker was wrong, his views prevailed, with the result that the 1973-convened Convention on Illegal Trade in Endangered Species (CITES) took two years to put African elephants even on Appendix II of their listings, and another twelve years to recognize Douglas-Hamilton's warnings of imminent extinction and to upgrade them to Appendix I. (The Asian elephant had been placed on Appendix I straight away.) This was too late for hundreds of thousands of elephants. Moreover, the composition of elephant societies

A road sign in one of the many South African private reserves to have recently acquired translocated elephants.

was becoming severely skewed by the selective offtake of tuskers and large females.

A second sticking-point was that CITES in any case had no legal teeth, even amongst its 113 signatory nations. There were too many loopholes in its regulations, and little chance of finally distinguishing on the ground between 'legal' and 'illegal', 'worked' and 'unworked' ivory. (A recent report estimated that 94 per cent of ivory merchandise sold on eBay, the world's largest online auctioneer, was in fact illegal; eBay has now banned it.) More damagingly still, CITES was at times partly funded by, and therefore reluctant to alienate, ivory traders themselves. Douglas Chadwick discovered, as he relates in his excellent, frightening book *The Fate of the Elephant*, that in the late 1980s Japanese ivory merchants were feeding a kind of self-imposed tax on their products into CITES coffers. The Japanese were at that time particularly concerned to preserve an icon of Japanese musical culture: the *baachi*, an enormous plectron for the *shamison* lute, carved from a single tusk and producing an allegedly unique, culturally sacrosanct sound. Moreover, CITES director Eugene LaPointe had for years been exploiting legal loopholes to release tons of 'stock-piled' African ivory to Far Eastern entrepreneurs. To this day CITES is, rightly or wrongly, regularly accused by its detractors of actively abetting the trade rather than suppressing it. In July 2008 CITES succumbed to pressure from southern African nations and permitted them to release large stockpiles of ivory onto the open market, in the face of East African protests that this is likely to reinvigorate poaching. As it is, recent estimates are that in Africa the elephant death rate from poaching is already 8 per cent higher than it was twenty years ago.[6]

That said, as a number of countries signed up, the 1989 CITES ban on ivory trading, though it may not have been the only factor, seemed to result in a marked downturn in the volume of trade. However, this is possibly to miscalculate the amounts that inevitably circulate clandestinely, especially coming out of war-torn zones like southern Sudan and southern Angola. In the latter case, South African military forces in the 1980s took advantage of the chaos to poach and sell tusks on the black market. One report claimed that Angola's UNITA forces killed 100,000 elephants in order to pay for South Africa's military support. There is ongoing argument, then, about the extent to which an international ban merely drives the trade underground, and to what extent the open economization of elephant products, as has been practised to some local benefit in Zimbabwe and South Africa, is a better option.

The Douglas-Hamilton vs Parker dispute also highlighted a third problem: determining the extent to which other factors – international prices, waves of fashion, local politics, cultural inhibitions, modes of land use, poverty and both short- and longer-term ecological changes – might also play a role in reducing elephant populations. Since elephant distribution is now perforce fragmented, each population suffers and enjoys a unique mix of influences, threats and benefits, so a blanket policy forged by international organizations is unlikely to cater adequately for all situations. This underlies, on a broad scale, the southern African/East African split. Asian elephant guru Raman Sukumar, in his memoir *Elephant Days and Nights*, captures the complexities succinctly:

We live in a world of contradictions, where there is an obscene disparity between rich and poor, and where there are tugs and pulls in every direction, where there is a need for the have-nots to catch up with the haves, and a need for both modernization and conservation. As we recklessly continue to assault the earth's living systems, our hearts are sometimes moved by the plight of the more charismatic creatures – the whooping crane, the tiger, the elephant. Often the plethora of issues, political, social, economic and biological, involved in the effort to save a species, makes us throw up our hands in despair.[7]

On one issue, at least, almost all parties agree: an overwhelming factor is the loss of habitat and freedom of movement right across elephant ranges. In Asia, this has been much more important than ivory poaching – though there, too, devastating poaching has happened, and continues to happen. To highlight this, we can note the remarkable career of the poacher Veerappan in southern India. Armed with weapons spilling over from the Sri Lanka conflict, this elusive gangster was long wanted for several murders of police and rangers. He had a more sophisticated intelligence network than the authorities, and the status of a kind of local Robin Hood among some rural communities. He and a network of poachers like him had a marked effect on the proportion of large breeding males amongst southern India's elephant populations. Latest surveys indicate that since Veerappan's demise, the number of elephants in his Kamataka stamping-ground has risen again from about 4,500 to 6,000. On the other hand, recent reports characterize ivory poaching in Jaipur province as 'rampant'.

Loss of habitat has had a number of negative effects. One is that increasingly isolated, inbreeding populations of elephants may show genetic defects over time. In Asia, there has been very little in the way of moving breeding elephants between groups. In southern Africa it is more common, though tremendously expensive. (This is not helped by loss of diversity even amongst domesticated elephants, which are almost as much in danger of extinction as their wild counterparts. In one estimate, Thailand had around 100,000 domesticated elephants at the turn of the twentieth century, but today there are a mere 3,800.)

Most importantly, habitat constriction has everywhere entailed an increase in human–elephant conflict. Elephants have, of course, always raided humans' tasty crops. Who wouldn't be tempted by such handy concentrations of nutrients? This is especially widespread in Asia, where human populations are highest and national parks both small and poorly protected. In India's Assam state, for example, some 7,000 out of 20,000 square kilometres of forest reserve are occupied by illegal settlers. Villagers – who otherwise venerate Ganesh – resort to poison, gunfire or dangling live wires from overhead electricity cables to try to deter elephantine raiders from their rice paddies. One dead elephant was daubed with the angry graffito, 'Dhan Chor Bin Laden' ('Rice Thief Bin Laden'). In July 2007 one Assam headman, Rosan Sangma, reported 27 local homes destroyed by elephants that year so far, and another devastating raid by a 90-strong cohort of elephants. During this same period, a number of incidents were reported involving elephants in Nepal, either poached or killed by farmers. Indeed, any given month's reports show a dramatic, paradoxical opposition between those lamenting destructive agricultural incidents in both Asia and Africa, and those sentimentally obsessing over births or deaths of individual elephants in captivity in the West.

Hence, in many areas, a new emphasis in conservation is on trying to manage human–elephant conflict, and to find ways in which preserving wildlife that is otherwise dangerous can benefit rural communities. As Kenya's Richard Leakey has realized, the welfare of human and natural populations are mutually reliant:

Two young elephant bulls practising dominance behaviour on the River Chobe, Botswana.

Giving up natural spaces and killing animal species will not bring prosperity . . . Clean air, clean water, plentiful forests, and a human population that is well fed, educated, and reasonably affluent is our goal in Kenya. Saving the elephants is symbolic – a means to achieve these greater objectives.[8]

The CAMPFIRE project (Communal Areas Management Programme for Indigenous Resources) in Zimbabwe was one pioneering effort, directing hunting and tourism revenue directly back into local schools and clinics. Successful in several instances, the projects are now running foul of the collapse of law and order under Robert Mugabe: none other than the vaunted 'Presidential Herd' of elephants in north-western

Matetsi, ostensibly specially protected by Mugabe's own presidential decree, is threatened with poaching organized by local warlords or even government ministers in cahoots with overseas hunters. Other efforts are being directed to deterrence – using walls, trenches, electrified fencing or fields of repellent chilli plants. The newest experiment is broadcasting recordings of bee swarms, which elephants are said to abhor.

There are elephant victims of other kinds of territorial conflict, too: those that inadvertently step on landmines in war zones. This has surfaced particularly in Myanmar's border regions where rebel groups contest the ruling junta. In 1999 one elephant in particular was rescued, named Motala. At the specialized elephant hospital in Lampang in northern Thailand, Motala became a global media star as she underwent amputation after stepping on an anti-personnel mine. Six years later the leg was able to take the world's first elephantine prosthesis –an ironic reversal, one might say, of the artificial shoulder of ivory said to have been granted by the ancient Greek gods to Pelops of Phrygia.

One thing is certain: worldwide, elephants have been cramped into areas too small for them – and paradoxically, where management and protection is successful, the pressure of their own numbers is proving to be a major headache. It's difficult, though, to know what those numbers entail. As elephant biologist Rudi van Aarde has said, 'If we cannot agree on the numbers we are dealing with in the first place, it is small wonder that the debates surrounding elephant management are clouded in uncertainty'.[9] Before one can begin to debate how many elephants there 'ought' to be in a given area, one needs to know how many there already are. And that's not as easy to determine as it might seem. Not only are elephants famously elusive, melting into thick vegetation or rough terrain like great grey ghosts, but they also often wander back and forth across international borders, making firm counts – which are usually conducted country by country – particularly difficult.

In Asia, estimates of elephants left in the wild range from 40,000 to over 52,000. In some regions, monitoring has been closer than in others. In South India, for instance, one can now access the results of a close census done in 2002 area by area – though even here researchers doubt the accuracy of their methods, and some leeway of doubt is built in.[10] India as a whole now harbours between 26,000 and 35,000 elephants in the wild, distributed in fragmented habitats over some three million square kilometres of range territory. This is an increase since 1980, when there were an estimated 15,600 wild elephants (though some of the increase may be due to advances in monitoring techniques). South India holds the most (some 15,000), followed by the north-east (about 11,000).

Twelve other Asian countries still have small elephant populations, ranging from a probable maximum of some 4,500 in Myanmar, 3,000 in each of Sri Lanka, Sumatra, Indonesia and Thailand, down to only a hundred-odd in Vietnam. Nepal, Bhutan, Bangladesh, China, Laos and Cambodia each probably have only a few hundred wild elephants left. These are the tattered remnants of a population that once presumably numbered in the hundreds of thousands, if not millions: there are simply no reliable estimates. So isolated are most populations that there are serious implications for genetic diversity, and ecologists are talking about applying principles of 'island ecology' to them.

In this respect, the position in Sumatra can stand for the whole. Already an island, it carries yet smaller 'islands' of threatened elephant groups (which, you will recall, may have evolved into a distinct subspecies). No reliable surveys were done until recently. Now, of 44 separate elephant groups discerned in the 1980s – then estimated at maybe 4,500 individuals – several seem to have disappeared. Counts in two of the main parks, Bukit Barisan Selatan and Way Kambas, produced population estimates of only 498 and 180 elephants, respectively. Though there has been some poaching, the major threats remain habitat loss to logging and other agriculture; the Wildlife Conservation Society estimates that, at the present rate, 70 per cent of Bukit park will be agricultural by 2010. The usual strategy against crop-raiding elephants here is to ask the government to remove them, and a number of Elephant Training Centres have been set up to receive these captives. Researcher Joanne Reilly once drove 1,500 kilometres with a three-month-old elephant baby, left behind after a crop raid, to the Centre at Sebanga Duri. Little Wiwin, as she was named, seemed to flourish for a time, but finally died while being airlifted to a zoo in Java. Her fate is depressingly symbolic.[11] There is, in short, very little effective safety for the remaining elephants, though Indonesia has technically protected them since 1931.

As for Africa, there is general but vague agreement that, despite everything, there were several million elephants left in 1900. Estimates were very rough then, and are only somewhat less so today, despite extensive aerial surveys, dung counts and variously sophisticated extrapolative models. Elephants range over some 22 per cent of Africa's 23 million square kilometres, but only a third of that range falls within protected areas; only half of their range has ever been actually surveyed, and even there some of the data is already a decade old. IUCN's latest 2007 survey, then, lists its estimates under 'definite', 'probable', 'possible' and frankly 'speculative', coming up with a total of some 472,000 elephants, Africa-wide. Of these, southern (300,000) and East Africa (137,000) account for the vast majority. In the

Man travelling on an elephant, India.

dense forests of Central Africa, elephants are not only more difficult to find, but are also less well protected in law and in practice. West Africa's populations, down to around 7,500, are in even worse shape.

Most West African elephants are in Ghana and Mali, but the scattered populations, split between forest and savannah dwellers, are often cross-border migrants: the largest single herd spans Benin, Togo, Burkina Faso and Niger in its wanderings. The semi-desert Sahel is now devoid of elephants apart from one 500-strong contingent, whose plight stands as symbolic of most elephant groups. Until the 1980s, human–elephant conflict in this region south of Timbuktu was manageable, since most people were Tuareg or related nomads, moving, much as the elephants did, over 500 kilometres or more, following seasonal water and forage. Now, however, as the region dries out, human and livestock populations are increasing and becoming more sedentary around the rare oases, so that the elephant migration routes are in danger of being cut off. As so often, governments' capacity to coordinate and implement conservation strategies is weak, despite various international conservation agreements such as that signed under the local economic union, ECOWAS. So it's mostly Western agencies such as Save the Elephants that are here tracking elephants with radio collars and spearheading negotiations with human communities to keep those routes open and the elephant population viable.[12]

Central Africa is covered extensively by equatorial forests, harbouring mainly the *cyclotis* forest elephant. As a result, one of the major threats is logging, both legal and illegal, which has opened up once inaccessible areas to ivory poaching and the bushmeat trade. A 2004 CITES survey called MIKE (Monitoring the Illegal Killing of Elephants) assessed most protected areas in these countries, showing the Democratic Republic of Congo and Gabon to have the bulk of Central Africa's population. But the actual levels of predation on elephants remains difficult to calculate. It is certain, though, that the devastating civil war in the DRC, as in neighbouring Rwanda, has resulted in extensive habitat loss, poverty-driven meat consumption, and a constant supply of illegal ivory through the main entrepôts in the DRC, Ivory Coast and Central African Republic. (The entrepreneurial descendants of Joseph Conrad's infamous character Kurtz, in his 1899 novella of the Congo, *Heart of Darkness*, continue to ply their trade.)

East Africa – mainly Kenya and Tanzania – has its own conservation story. The names Serengeti, Ngorongoro, Masai Mara and Tsavo are virtually synonymous with elephants; no elephant picture, perhaps, is better known than that of peaceful pachyderms making their way across the yellow savannah with the snow-capped dome of Kilimanjaro suspended airily in the background. A large proportion of researchers and activists have cut their teeth here and devoted themselves to elephants in this region: the pioneering Douglas-Hamiltons; Daphne Sheldrick, who continues to run her elephant orphanage near Nairobi; David Western; Joyce Poole and Cynthia Moss; Katy Payne, who pioneered the recording of the elephants' infrasonic communications; and the redoubtable Richard Leakey, who built up the Kenya Wildlife Service and who titled his 2001 memoir *Wildlife Wars: My Battle to Save Kenya's Elephants.*

Leakey's account tells a grimly familiar tale: of poaching for ivory and killing poachers; of corrupt and inefficient governments; of the pressure of human poverty coupled with habitat erosion. Poaching concerned Leakey most: he witnessed Kenya's elephants reduced from perhaps 100,000 in 1979 to a fifth of that in a decade. Tanzania's Selous National Park held a similar number, and suffered similarly devastating losses. After the elephant was placed on the endangered list and ivory trading was suppressed, however, the populations have partially recovered – at least in Tanzania (numbering in 2007 some 108,000), Kenya (23,000) and Uganda (2,300); fragmentary populations in Sudan, Somalia, Eritrea, Ethiopia and Rwanda remain in precarious and poorly known conditions. Leakey's efforts included organizing a famous and controversial public burning of Kenya's huge stockpile of ivory in 1989 (emulated in 2007 by Chad, with much less fanfare). Yet today, only Tanzania has a coordinated elephant conservation strategy in place.

With the elephants' partial recovery in many regions, however, human–elephant conflict has increased. In some areas, managers like Ian Parker began to argue that it was not poaching that was the major problem, but habitat constriction;

it was not that too many elephants were being lost, but that there were too many for the land available. Hence the controversial policy of 'culling' was first instituted as a management strategy in Tsavo in the early 1960s, and Parker himself organized culls in Murchison Falls National Park from 1965 onwards. They called it 'cropping for scientific purposes', and generated funds by processing and selling elephant products. Peter Beard was one big-game hunter who joined these culls, documenting them in his frankly gruesome book, *The End of the Game*.

Population issues are even more intense in southern Africa, which has effected a remarkable turnaround in elephant populations. Here, too, the elephant has become the most prominent 'keystone' symbol of wider conservation efforts – just as it was once the primary symbol of the hunter's prowess. The allegedly 'natural' urge of hirsute male humans to hunt is being repackaged in one novel concept: 'green hunting'. In a reserve adjoining Kruger, hunters are paying to dart tuskers with anaesthetic, prior to radio-collaring them, instead of killing them. Somewhat like their nineteenth-century forebear hunters, they can both get their 'bag' and contribute to science. The 'conversion rate' from lethal to green hunting is yet to become clear, though, and some animal rights activists are opposed even to this milder form of earning revenue from elephants.

Today, a big tusker signifies, rather than a potential dead trophy, great age and great genes; its survival is therefore a reflection of great conservation practice. In Kenya, the limelight was captured by the legendary Ahmed of Marsabit; in South Africa, the tuskers of Kruger have captured most imaginations – as in Anthony Hall-Martin's book *The Magnificent Seven*, illustrated with paintings by Paul Bosman, and the even more recent *Great Tuskers of Africa*. The tuskers are named, tracked and mourned when they die, almost as if they were people.

Paul Bosman is one artist fascinated by the 'Great Tuskers' of Kruger National Park, South Africa.

The story of Addo, the reserve near my home which I mentioned at the beginning of this book, is a good example of the southern African turnaround. During the course of the eighteenth and nineteenth centuries the whole of the then Cape Colony of South Africa, like much of the subcontinent, had been denuded of elephant. A small population survived into the twentieth century in the densest of Addo's euphorbia thickets, an understandably wary and aggressive group that periodically raided the burgeoning citrus farms along the nearby Sundays river. A professional hunter, one Major Pretorius, was hired to eradicate them. By 1925 Pretorius had reduced them to (he thought) 16 – others believed there might still be as many as 50. At any event, both Pretorius's stomach and public opinion were turning, and it was decided rather to fence the surviving elephants off into a reserve, enclosing them behind a robust barrier of railway sleepers and cable.

Today, Addo contains some 400 elephants, mostly scions of the original group, genetically leavened by some imports from Kruger, and their range has been hugely expanded to some five times the original area, as neighbouring farms have been bought up and added. In this respect, too, Addo reflects the wider history of southern Africa's wildlife parks, from shaky beginnings to present-day, tourist-driven expansion. Great efforts are being made today to create so-called Peace Parks, trans-frontier conjoinings of existing reserves and corridors, which may do much to relieve population pressures within the reserves.

South Africa's flagship reserve, the Kruger National Park, began in the late 1800s as a hunting preserve for the white political elite. (It was not, as is popularly believed, instigated by the crusty President, Oom Paul Kruger, but only named after him; in fact, he was downright obstructive.) Only subsequently was it expanded to an area the size of Belgium, displacing large

Among the members of this allomother group in Addo, communications by sound, touch and gesture are enormously complex – a factor in the culling debate.

Elephants damaging vegetation: this 'big-headed' elephant, uprooting a tree, from an unknown British journal, *c.* 1890, preserves inaccurate artistic convention.

numbers of indigenous peoples in the process, and dedicated to rebuilding animal populations rather than plundering them. There were almost no elephants in Kruger at its inauguration (there may never have been very many); there are now some 14,000. This, according to many ecologists, is more than the ecosystem can bear. Managers and ecologists saw hundreds of baobab and acacia trees being fatally stripped or knocked down, sometimes more for display than for food, with obvious knock-on effects on many other tree-dependent species, from herbivorous bushbuck down to vultures and insects. Elephants, the common cry became, were 'environmental engineers', capable of 'reducing' large areas to grassland in short order.

Hence, during the 1960s a notional 'carrying capacity' of 7,000 elephants was established for Kruger. This was admittedly little more than a hazardous guess (one elephant per square mile, more or less), since insufficient longitudinal studies existed upon which to base any figure at all. The whole notion of 'carrying capacity' was, arguably inappropriately, transferred from domestic livestock models. No one really knows, for example, to what extent elephants might self-regulate birth-rates once suitable vegetation thins out or if artificial water points are reduced, or to what extent biodiversity might really be damaged in the long term. The roughly 250 scientific papers so far published on this issue across the globe are split just about down the middle between those that proclaim irreversible damage to be blamed on elephants, and those that don't. There is simply no consensus.

You wouldn't believe it, to listen to some adamant park managers, and even some biologists. One problem is that, in effect, park managers have a certain vision of what a given park 'ought' to look like, what other species it 'should' contain, and want to manage the game accordingly. This view, though nowadays couched in the language of 'biodiversity', is fundamentally static and aesthetic (an aspect once openly acknowledged in a 1989 booklet, *Elephant Management in Zimbabwe*). In fact, ecosystems change radically over time; there is no single 'right' baseline. There is as yet very little understanding of longer-term oscillations and changes, though pollen-based studies in Tsavo, which give us some idea of vegetation regimes over a 1,500-year period, look like a promising start. But it would appear that 'the growing awareness amongst academic and applied ecologists of the dynamic nature of ecosystems has seldom been matched amongst wildlife management authorities'.[13] Moreover, because the pressure to cull has so often been linked to the sale of elephant products, ostensibly to raise money for further conservation, the suspicion has arisen that 'culling' is 'essentially an ivory harvesting programme operating at maximum sustainable yield'.[14] Possible earnings in 2005 were estimated by The Earth organization at R6.5 million for every 800 elephants killed – a tidy sum.

'It's nature's way of keeping numbers down!': cartoonist Rose Rigden solves the population dilemma.

At any rate, *perceived* overpopulation in Kruger precipitated an annual 'cull' of up to a thousand elephants a year, feeding a huge but discreet processing factory on the edge of the park. Some 17,000 elephants were killed between 1966 and 1995, when animal rights activists forced a moratorium. At first, rifles alone were used, then a muscle relaxant named succinylcholine chloride (Scoline), which downed the animal but left it conscious until shot. Condemned for causing unnecessary mental distress, it was discontinued elsewhere, but South Africa continued to use it until the culling was stopped. Animal rights organizations like the International Fund for Animal Welfare (IFAW) have maintained that the practice is 'cruel, unethical and scientifically unsound'.[15] Since then, a more subtle and interesting strategy has been followed, dividing Kruger into several zones, each with a different approach, from hunting some elephants to leaving them entirely alone. This reflects the emergence of 'patchiness' as a mantra for ecologists wishing to preserve biodiversity. It remains to be seen, however, what the long-term outcome of this might be. In the meantime, the prospect of culling has reared its head again and generated intense debate, amongst politicians and philosophers as well as ecologists and managers. On 1 May 2008 the eighteen-year moratorium on culling in South Africa was lifted, albeit hedged about with strict conditions. It is surely the saddest paradox in all conservation history that while all over the world desperate efforts are made to save individual elephants, there are places where it is seen to be necessary to kill off literally thousands.

The culling debate is a complex business. It's riven, first, by a perceived gulf between the 'pragmatic', scientific, managerial ecologists and the 'sentimental' (generally Western) animal rights and public-opinion lobbies. The first group tends to think in statistics, the second in terms of suffering individuals. This division reappears everywhere. Richard Leakey, for example, has been condemned as 'emotional' by some ecologists. Early on, researchers like the Douglas-Hamiltons and Cynthia Moss were scorned by scientists for daring to *name* their subjects, rather than assign numbers. And here is Masakazu Kashio, a forestry officer opening an important FAO workshop on domesticated Asian elephants in Bangkok in 2001, exhorting the participants to be forthright, but asking that attendees

> please keep in mind one important point, which is that your statements should be scientific, logical, rational and either supported by research works or facts that you have directly observed or experienced. Please avoid political propaganda, emotional arguments, and personal ego, because these are neither appropriate nor constructive . . .[16]

It's the division between Dame Daphne Sheldrick's view that 'the very human intelligence' and compassion of elephants 'is something that the scientific community has always been slow to acknowledge' and ecologist Paul Manger's warning that 'elephants are elephants, not big grey humans'. Manger advocates instead 'a detailed study of the elephant's brain, which will provide a strong scientific platform for interpreting elephant behaviour.'[17] Progress in the debate seems unlikely unless some way is found of overcoming this false dichotomy.

Scientists and managers are not, of course, entirely lacking in emotion. It's fascinating to see how culling methods have changed over the years along with a deepening understanding of elephant sensitivities. Not only was it recognized that killing off selected males was not having the population-suppressing effects the managers intended, but it was also observed that the elephants left behind suffered 'psychological trauma' much as humans do. (Such observations found their way even into that most prestigious of scientific journals, *Nature*.[18]) Hence managers adopted the tactic of slaughtering entire groups, from the matriarch down to the smallest calf. Now even this has been complicated by the knowledge that other groups, sometimes tens of miles away, pick up the infrasonic distress of the targeted families and can show signs of disturbance. It is these 'emotional' characteristics that have also galvanized wealthy animal welfare organizations to pressure governments to halt culling, though a number of mainstream NGOs like the Worldwide Fund for Nature and the Wildlife and Environment Society of South Africa continue cautiously to support it, if only as a last resort.

One has to feel for the managers, who after all have to do *something* – and making the decision to do nothing might mean at some point, during a bad drought perhaps, the terrible sight of hundreds of elephants visibly dying of thirst – what would *that* do to the tourism business?

Much of the debate has focused on possible alternatives to culling. These are limited: range expansion, translocation and contraception. The opportunities for both expansion and expensive translocations have already been all but exhausted in southern Africa. Although private reserves have proliferated recently, and a few hundred elephants have been moved to parks like Addo or to private estates, ranging from forest sanctuaries near Knysna to the semi-desert of the Karoo, there is not much more space available. Not unless lots of people move instead. It's even tighter in Asia, where 'elephant corridors' between suitable habitats have been mooted, but seem unlikely to be implemented.

Contraception remains a focus for intensive research. Various drugs, particularly porcine zona pellucida (PZP), have been proposed, but none has been adequately tested, and the prospect of success remains dubious. Darting selected females to prevent conception, for instance, would be stressful and have to happen regularly: in an area like Kruger, where the animals are difficult to find anyway, the close monitoring necessary would be all but impossible, and the expense is prohibitive. No one knows what the social consequences for the elephants would be if, say, some females and not others were given contraceptives or permanently sterilized. Contraception might keep birth rates down, but would not reduce absolute numbers, so the problem of impact on vegetation remains. It is probably viable only in very small, tightly controlled populations. However, it is being actively implemented, in conjunction with selective culling, in South Africa's Tembe Elephant Park, for one.

So what of the future? In some ways, the prospect for the elephant isn't wholly gloomy. In some places, populations are healthy, albeit only in relation to the resources within severely restricted ranges. Scientific knowledge of elephants and their needs has expanded exponentially. Hence better legislation is gradually being implemented world-wide. Zoos and circuses are having to clean up their acts radically. There are now more dedicated organizations than one can wave a trunk at: Elephant Care International, Golden Triangle Asian Elephant Foundation, Friends of the Asian Elephant, Save the Elephants, Elephants for Africa Forever, and dozens more. Awareness – of alternatives to ivory, for example – is making headway, though not yet sufficiently in the Far East. Domestication of African elephants for touristic purposes, though itself controversial, is at least making the electrifying touch of an elephant available to more people, with some positive conservation spin-offs. In West and Central Africa some progress is being made in establishing

The 'cute' factor in the lightly furred baby elephant can result in accusations of 'sentimentalizing' elephants.

and policing better-protected areas. More and more effort is being devoted to finding workable ways of allowing elephants and rural communities to coexist.

For all that, the juggernaut of human expansion seems unstoppable; habitat loss and unsustainable exploitation will remain continual threats to elephant survival for the foreseeable future. While appeals to biodiversity and related scientific observations are vital, it seems to me that it's a simple compassion for the fate of an extraordinary creature that will ultimately have the greatest sway. So I'd like to leave the final word to novelist Romain Gary, from that odd mix of early conservationism and Gallic existential gloom, his oft-cited novel *The Roots of Heaven*:

'I defy anyone to look upon elephants without a sense of wonder. Their very enormity, their clumsiness, their giant stature, represent a mass of liberty that sets you dreaming. They're . . . yes, they're the last individuals . . .'

'No, mademoiselle, I don't capture elephants. I content myself with living among them. I like them. I like looking at them, listening to them, watching them on the horizon. To tell you the truth, I'd give anything to become an elephant myself.'[19]

Timeline of the Elephant

c. 60 million BC	*c.* 40 million BC	*c.* 24 million BC	*c.* 3 million BC
Probiscidae and hyraxes part from common ancestor	Oldest Proboscidae fossils	Miocene era produces deinotheres, stegodons and gomphotheres	Asian and African elephant *clades* part

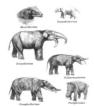

c. 3000 BC	*c.* 1500–1000 BC	347 BC	221 BC
Asian elephants first captured and trained	*Mahabharata* and *Ramayana* mythic elephant tales compiled	Alexander the Great confronts Porus' elephants at Hydaspes	Hannibal crosses the Alps with his elephants

c. 1880–1900	1882	1899
Heyday of Great White Hunters like Neumann and Selous	'Jumbo' taken from London to USA by Barnum circuses	Largest recorded elephant tusks collected from Kenyan bull

c. 2 million BC	*c.* 25,000 BC	*c.* 17,000 BC	*c.* 11,000 BC
Mini Ice Age prompts an elephantid explosion	Earliest Bushman rock art in southern Africa includes elephants	Mammoths painted on cave walls in France	Mammoths extinct in North America, through combination of climatic and human influence

c. AD 600	1552	1811	*c.* 1850
Ganesh god-figure evolves under Aryan influence	Elephant 'Sulayman' given to Emperor Maximilian	Family Proboscidae formed by taxonomist Illger	Piano production rockets, launching massive ivory trade

1931	1951	1973	1989
First Babar story published	Serengeti Park proclaimed, parallelling that of other great elephant reserves	Asian elephant placed on CITES Appendix I	CITES announces ivory trade ban

References

1 PROBOSCIDAE

1 Haruo Saegusa, Yupa Thasod and Benjavun Ratanasthien, 'Notes on Asian Stegodontids', *Quaternary International*, CXXVI–CXXVIII (2005), pp. 31–48.
2 Cited in Raman Sukumar, The Living Elephants: Evolutionary Ecology, Behaviour and Conservation (Oxford, 2003), p. 18.
3 Jeheskel Shoshani, 'Understanding Probiscidean Evolution: A Formidable Task', Trends in Ecology and Evolution, vol. XIII/12 (1998), pp. 480–87.
4 Eric Scigliano, Love, War and Circuses: The Age-old Relationship Between Elephants and Humans (New York, 2002), pp. 20–21.
5 Robert Delort, The Life and Lore of the Elephant (London, 1992), p. 130.
6 Ibid., p. 131.
7 www.situ.ru/culture/museum/mamont/index_eng.shtml (accessed February 2007).
8 www.science.psu.edu/alert/schuster12-2005.htm (accessed 3 August 2008).
9 www.exn.ca/mammoth/Gods.cfm (accessed February 2007).
10 Delort, The Life and Lore of the Elephant, p. 131.
11 Michael Oard, 'The Extinction of the Woolly Mammoth: Was it a Quick Freeze?', Technical Journal, vol. XV/3, pp. 24–34, www.answersingenesis.org/Home/Area/Magazines/tj/docs/tj14 _3-mo_mammoth.pdf.

12 Sukumar, *The Living Elephants*, p. 29.
13 Ibid., p. 43; Gary Haynes, 'Mammoth Landscapes: Good Country for Hunter-Gatherers', *Quaternary International*, CXLII–CXLIII (2006), pp. 30–43.
14 'Were Mammoths Killed off by a Comet?', *Economist*, 383 (24 May 2007), p. 94.
15 Shoshani, 'Understanding Probiscidean Evolution'. See also Shoshani and Pascal Tassy, 'Advances in Proboscidean Taxonomy and Classification', *Quaternary International*, CXXVI–CXXVIII, pp. 5–20.
16 Josh Trapani and Daniel C. Fisher, 'Discriminating Proboscidean Taxa Using Features of the Schreger Pattern in Tusk Dentin', *Journal of Archaeological Science*, XXX/4 (2003), pp. 429 38.
17 Nancy E. Todd, 'Reanalysis of African *Elephas recki*: Implications for Time, Space and Taxonomy', *Quaternary International*, CXXVI–CXXVIII (2005), pp. 65–72.
18 Sukumar, *The Living Elephants*, p. 52.
19 Ibid., p. 54.

2 AN ASTOUNDING PHYSIOLOGY

1 Heathcote Williams, *Sacred Elephant* (New York, 1989), p. 78.
2 E. J. Raubenheimer et al., 'Histogenesis of the Chequered Pattern of Ivory of the African Elephant (*Loxodonta Africana*)', *Archives of Oral Biology*, XLIII/12 (1998), pp. 969–77. See also F. Burragato et al., 'New Forensic Tool for the Identification of Elephant or Mammoth Ivory', *Forensic Science International*, XCVI/2–3 (1998), pp. 189–96.
3 Katy Payne, *Silent Thunder: The Hidden Voice of Elephants* (Jeppestown, 1998), pp. 13–14.
4 Paul Bosman and Anthony Hall-Martin, *The Magnificent Seven: And Other Great Tuskers of the Kruger National Park* (Cape Town, 1994), p. 50.
5 Polly K. Phillips and James Edward Heath, 'Heat Exchange by the Pinna of the African Elephant (*Loxodonta africana*)', *Comparative*

Biochemistry and Physiology, Part A: Physiology, CI/4 (1992), pp. 693–9.

6 Cited in Eric Scigliano, *Love, War and Circuses: The Age-Old Relationship between Elephants and Humans* (New York, 2002), p. 20.

7 J. H. Williams, *Bandoola* (London, 1953), p. 79.

8 Cynthia Moss, *Elephant Memories: Thirteen Years in the Life of an Elephant Family* (Chicago, IL, 2000), p. 128.

9 Anthony Hall-Martin, 'A Life Spent in the Conservation Game', *Getaway* (September 2000), p. 57.

10 See Milad Doueihi, 'Elephantine Marriage: The Elephant and Devout Table Manners', *Modern Language Notes*, CVI (1991), pp. 720–28.

11 'Making Magic Work', amerindea.com/symbol-elephant.html.

12 Karen McComb et al., 'Long-distance Communication of Acoustic Cues to Social Identity in African Elephants', *Animal Behaviour*, LXV/2 (2003), pp. 317–29.

13 Chris Mann, *Kites* (Cape Town, 1990), p. 14.

14 Iain Douglas-Hamilton and Oria Douglas-Hamilton, *Among the Elephants* (London, 1975), p. 265.

15 'Elephants Recognize their Mirror Image', *New Scientist*, CXCII/2576 (4 November 2006), p. 17.

16 Daphne Sheldrick, 'A Kindred Species', *Africa Geographic*, XIV/3 (2006), p. 26.

17 Paul Manger, 'Elephants are Elephants', *Africa Geographic*, XIV/3 (2006), p. 25.

3 REPRESENTING ELEPHANTS

1 Michael Chapman, ed., *The New Century of South African Poetry* (Johannesburg, 2005), p. 13.

2 Judith Gleason, ed., *Leaf and Bone: African Praise-poems* (New York, 1980), p. 123.

3 Cited in Stephen Alter, *Elephas Maximus: A Portrait of the Indian Elephant* (Orlando, FL, 2004), p. 38.

4 Ibid., p. 34.

5 Robert Delort, *The Life and Lore of the Elephant* (London, 1992), p. 48.

6 Ibid., p. 68.

7 Richard Carrington, *Elephants* (London, 1958), p. 249.

8 See 'Heart of an Elephant', *Mail & Guardian* [Johannesburg], 'Friday' section, 9–15 November (2007), p. 5.

9 Mordikai Hamutyinei and Albert Plangger, *Tsumo-Shumo* (Gweru, 1987), pp. 5, 188, 234, 382.

10 *African Affairs*, LIII/213 (1954), p. 332.

11 Alexander McCall Smith, *The Girl Who Married a Lion* (London, 1989).

12 Anon., in *Words that Circle Words: A Choice of South African Oral Poetry*, ed. Jeff Opland (Parklands, 1992), p. 169.

13 Delort, *The Life and Lore of the Elephant*, p. 155.

14 Arthur H. Neumann, *Elephant Hunting in East Equatorial Africa* [1898] (Bulawayo, 1982), p. 107.

15 Wilbur Smith, *Elephant Song* (London, 1991), pp. 9–11.

16 Dalene Matthee, *Circles in a Forest* (Harmondsworth, 1984), p. 71. Matthee wrote several elephant-related novels set in the Knysna forest.

17 Enid Blyton, 'Preface', *Jean de Brunhoff: Tales of Babar* [1941] (London, 1947), n.p.

18 www.timesonline.co.uk/tol/news/world/europe/article602843.ece.

19 www.brothersjudd.com/index.cfm/fuseaction/reviews.detail/ book_id/329.

20 Cited in Eric Scigliano, *Love, War and Circuses: The Age-Old Relationship between Elephants and Humans* (New York, 2002), p. 206.

21 Charles Dickens, *Hard Times* (Harmondsworth, 1990), pp. 20–21.

22 Virginia Woolf, *The Waves* (Harmondsworth, 1992), p. 6.

23 Vikram Seth, 'The Elephant and the Tragopan', in *Beastly Tales from Here and There* (London, 1994).

24 Harold Farmer, *Absence of Elephants* (Harare, 1990), pp. 34–5.

25 Douglas Livingstone, 'One Elephant', in *A Ruthless Fidelity: The*

Collected Poems of Douglas Livingstone, ed. Don Maclennan and Malcolm Hacksley (Jeppestown, 2004), p. 99.

26 Heathcote Williams, *Sacred Elephant* (New York, 1989), p. 76.

27 See www.pocketelephants.com.

28 See www.himandus.net/elephanteria.

29 Ivan Vladislavić, *The Restless Supermarket* (Cape Town, 2001), p. 1.

30 See www.creativepro.com/printerfriendly/story/20593.html.

31 See www.elephantcountryweb.com.

32 See www.dvdbeaver.com.

33 See Alter, *Elephas Maximus*, pp. 93–4.

4 USING ELEPHANTS

1 Karl Gröning and Martin Saller, eds, *Elephants: A Natural and Cultural History* (Cologne, 1998), p. 134.

2 Stephen Alter, *Elephas Maximus: A Portrait of the Indian Elephant* (Orlando, FL, 2004), p. 154.

3 Raman Sukumar, *The Living Elephants: Evolutionary Ecology, Behaviour and Conservation* (Oxford, 2003), pp. 72–4.

4 H. H. Scullard, *The Elephant in the Greek and Roman World*, p. 34.

5 Lyn de Alwis, 'Working Elephants', in *Illustrated Encyclopaedia of Elephants*, ed. S. K. Eltringham (London, 1997), p. 119.

6 Gröning and Saller, *Elephants*, p. 118.

7 Scullard, *The Elephant in the Greek and Roman World*, p. 132.

8 Ibid., p. 151.

9 J.R.R. Tolkien, *Lord of the Rings: The Two Towers* (London, 1979), p. 336.

10 Alter, *Elephas Maximus*, p. 157.

11 Gröning and Saller, *Elephants*, p. 142.

12 Ibid., p. 193.

13 J. H. Williams, *Bandoola* (London, 1953), p. 128.

14 See www.deselephantsetdeshommes.com for regular updates on such incidents.

15 Ted H. Friend, 'Behaviour of Picketed Circus Elephants', *Applied Animal Behaviour Studies*, LXII/1 (1991), pp. 73–88.

16 See www.elephantart.com

17 Sharon van Wyck, 'Back to Front', cited in *Earthyear*, 1 (2004), p. 58.

18 Eric Baratay and Elisabeth Hardouin-Fugier, *Zoo: A History of Zoological Gardens of the West* (London, 2004), p. 36.

19 www.asianelephants.net

20 'Zoos' Pachyderms Pack a Challenge', *Herald-Times* (20 June 2006).

21 Michael D. Lenswick, 'Who Belongs in the Zoo?', *Time* (19 June 2006), p. 50.

22 Baratay and Hardouin-Fugier, *Zoo*, p. 114.

23 Paul A. Rees, 'Asian Elephants in Zoos Face Global Extinction: Should Zoos Accept the Inevitable?' *Oryx*, xxxvii/1 (2003), pp. 20–22.

24 Jack Hanna, Director Emeritus, Columbus Zoo, from interview with *Centre Daily News* on 15 September 2006: www.asianelephants.com.

5 CONSERVATION

1 O. Beigbeder, *Ivory* (London, 1965).

2 See Ezio Bassani and William Fagg, *Africa and the Renaissance: Art in Ivory* (Munich, 1988).

3 Cited in Heathcote Williams, *Sacred Elephant* (New York, 1989), p. 156.

4 Cited in Martin Meredith, *Africa's Elephant: A Biography* (London, 2001), p. 72.

5 Cited in Robert Delort, *The Life and Lore of the Elephant* (London, 1992), p. 176.

6 'Ivory Poaching at Critical Levels: Elephants on Path to Extinction by 2020', *Science Daily* (1 August 2008): www.sciencedaily.com/releases/2008/07/080731140219.htm.

7 Raman Sukumar, *Elephant Days and Nights: Ten Years with the Indian Elephant* (Oxford, 1994), p. 163.

8 Richard E. Leakey, *Wildlife Wars: My Battle to Save Kenya's Elephants* (New York, 2001), p. x.

9 Rudi van Aarde, 'How Many is Too Many', *Africa Geographic*, xiv/3 (April 2006), p. 38.

10 See www.asiannature.org.

11 See www.bbc.co.uk/nature/animals/features/310feature1.shtml.

12 Carlton Ward, 'Restless Spirits of the Desert', *Africa Geographic*, xv/6 (July 2007), pp. 34–41.

13 Lindsey Gillson and Keith Lindsay, 'Ivory and Ecology: Changing Perspectives on Elephant Management and the International Trade in Ivory', *Environmental Science & Policy*, vi/5 (2003), p. 412.

14 Ibid., p. 417.

15 See www.ifaw.org/ifaw/dimages/custom/2_Publications /Elephants/ElephantCullDebate.pdf

16 www.fao.org/docrep/005/ad031e/ad031e05.htm#bm05.1.

17 Paul Manger, 'Elephants are Elephants'; Daphne Sheldrick, 'A Kindred Species', *Africa Geographic*, xiv/3 (April 2006), pp. 25–6.

18 See for instance *Nature*, 433 (2005), p. 807.

19 Romain Gary, *The Roots of Heaven* (London, 1958), pp. 108, 112.

Bibliography

Alter, Stephen, *Elephas Maximus: A Portrait of the Indian Elephant* (Orlando, FL, 2004)

Baratay, Eric, and Elisabeth Hardouin-Fugier, *Zoo: A History of Zoological Gardens of the West* (London, 2004)

Bosman, Paul, and Anthony Hall Martin, *The Magnificent Seven and the Other Great Tuskers of the Kruger National Park* (Cape Town, 1994)

Carrington, Richard, *Elephants* (London, 1958)

Chadwick, Douglas H., *The Fate of the Elephant* (London, 1992)

Delort, Robert, *The Life and Lore of the Elephant* (London, 1992)

Douglas-Hamilton, Iain, and Oria Douglas-Hamilton, *Among the Elephants* (London, 1975)

Eltringham, S. K., ed., *The Illustrated Encyclopaedia of Elephants* (London, 1997)

Gary, Romain, *The Roots of Heaven* (London, 1958)

Gavron, Jeremy, *The Last Elephant: An African Quest* (London, 1993)

Gowdy, Barbara, *The White Bone* (Toronto, 1998)

Gröning, Karl, and Martin Saller, eds, *Elephants: A Natural and Cultural History* (Cologne, 1998)

Hanks, John, *A Struggle for Survival: The Elephant Problem* (Cape Town, 1975)

Künkel, Reinhard, *African Elephants* (New York, 1999)

Leakey, Richard E., *Wildlife Wars: My Battle to Save Kenya's Elephants* (New York, 2001)

Meredith, Martin, *Africa's Elephant: A Biography* (London, 2001)

Moss, Cynthia, *Elephant Memories: Thirteen Years in the Life of an Elephant Family* (Chicago, IL, 2000)

Payne, Katy, *Silent Thunder: The Hidden Voice of Elephants* (Jeppestown, 1998)

Scigliano, Eric, *Love, War and Circuses: The Age-Old Relationship between Elephants and Humans* (New York, 2002)

Scullard, H. H., *The Elephant in the Greek and Roman World* (London, 1974)

Shand, Mark, *Queen of the Elephants* (London, 1996)

Smith, Wilbur, *Elephant Song* (London, 1991)

Sukumar, Raman, *Elephant Days and Nights: Ten Years with the Indian Elephant* (Oxford, 1994)

—, *The Living Elephants: Evolutionary Ecology, Behaviour and Conservation* (Oxford, 2003)

Sykes, Sylvia K., *The Natural History of the African Elephant* (London, 1971)

Williams, Heathcote, *Sacred Elephant* (New York, 1989)

Williams, J. H., *Elephant Bill* (London, 1950)

—, *Bandoola* (London, 1953)

Associations and Websites

ELEPHANT CARE INTERNATIONAL
166 Limo View lane, Hohenwald TN 38462, USA
www.elephantcare.org

FRIENDS OF THE ASIAN ELEPHANT
687/2 Ram-Indra Road
Soi 32, Tharaeng, Bangkhen, Bangkok, Thailand
www.elephant-soraida.com

INTERNATIONAL ELEPHANT FOUNDATION
PO Box 366, Asle TX 76098, USA
www.elephantconservation.org

INTERNATIONAL FUND FOR ANIMAL WELFARE
411 Main Street, PO Box 193
Yarmouth Port, MA 02675, USA
www.ifaw.org

IUCN AFRICAN ELEPHANT SPECIALIST GROUP
PO Box 68200, Nairobi, Kenya
www.iucn.org/afesg

IUCN SPECIES SURVIVAL COMMISSION
P/Bag x7, Claremont 7735, Cape Town, South Africa
www.iucn.org/ssc

SAVE THE ELEPHANTS
PO Box 54667, Nairobi, Kenya
www.save-the-elephants.com

www.asianelephant.net
Database of Asian elephants

www.blesele.com
Boon Lott's elephant sanctuary

www.deselephantsetdeshommes.org
Includes up-to-date daily incident reports

www.elephant.chabucto.us.ca/
African elephant bibliography

www.elephantcountryweb.com
Treaties, conventions and legislation, including CITES

www.elephant.elehost.com

www.helpingelephants.org
The Golden Triangle Asian Elephant Foundation

www.helptheelephants.com

www.himandus.net/elephanteria/index.html
Collects elephant images in advertising displays and logos

www.nal.usda.gov/awic/pubs/elephants/websites

www.natureartists.com/elephants.asp

Acknowledgements

Robert Bieder, author of *Bear* in this series, persuaded me to submit a proposal for *Elephant*. This book would not have happened without him, and he has continued to take a keen interest in the project. Quite apart from all the sources I've consulted, many people, some quite inadvertently or unknowingly, have personally helped make this book what it is. Those I can remember who have offered advice or support, lent or given me books, pointed me to sources, made gifts, or welcomed me into parks and sanctuaries, I list here, with apologies to any I've forgotten: Roy Bengis at Kruger National Park; Johan Binneman of the Albany Museum; Harold Farmer, Jayne Glover, Jenny Gon, Ron Hall, Pat Irwin; Malcolm Hacksley, Marike Beyers, Debbie Landman and the staff of the National English Literary Museum; Chris Kruger of the Elephant Sanctuary, Plettenberg Bay; Don Maclennan, Ben Maclennan, Chris Mann, Goenie Marsh, Jamie McGregor; Wayne Matthews and Bongani Tembe of Tembe Elephant Park; Dylan McGarry, Sam Naidu, Katja Rathofer, Ann Smailes, Peter Smailes, Mariss Stevens; Norman Travers of Imire, Zimbabwe; my mother, Jill Wylie; and Professor Rudi van Aarde. Special thanks are due to Professor Ric Bernard and Dr Dan Parker of Rhodes University for reading and correcting parts of the manuscript. Grateful thanks to Rhodes University for generous funding and professional support.

Photo Acknowledgements

The author and publishers wish to express their thanks to the below sources of illustrative material and/or permission to reproduce it.

Courtesy Susan Abraham: p. 103; © *Africa Geographic*: p. 111; photos by or courtesy of the author: pp. 8, 85, 103, 161, 166, 175; photo Greg Baker /AP Images, courtesy PictureNet: p. 23; photo © Steve Bloom/ stevebloom.com: p. 36; courtesy the artist (Paul Bosman): p. 174; photo © the Trustees of the British Museum, London: p. 8; photo by permission of David Coulson/TARA: pp. 66, 67; photo courtesy Sean Eriksen: p. 40 (foot); photo Eye Ubiquitous/Rex Features: p. 70; from William Fagg, *Nigerian Images* (London: Lund Humphries, 1990): p. 80 (top and lower left); photos courtesy David Ferris/Asian Elephant Art & Conservation Project, New York: pp. 146, 147; photo Charles Haynes: p. 69; photos Krishnanand Kamat/Kamat's Potpourri (www.kamat.com): pp. 68 (top), 71; Killie Campbell Collection: pp. 52, 58, 176; photos courtesy of the Library of Congress, Washington, DC: pp. 17, 28, 49, 72, 73, 77, 94, 107, 109, 113, 115, 121, 137, 141, 149, 156, 157; photo Herbert List: p. 80 (top and lower left); photo James McCauley/Rex Features: p. 170; photos courtesy John McKinnell: pp. 29, 30, 33, 35, 39, 42, 48, 55, 57, 110, 182; photo Ben Maclennan: p. 63; photo © Marie Mathelin/Roger-Viollet, courtesy Rex Features: p. 134 (foot); photo mdemon: p. 134 (top); photo courtesy Mana Meadows: p. 40 (top); Metropolitan Museum of Art, New York – photo Metropolitan Museum of Art Image Library: p. 75; photo A.E.W. Miles: p. 22; photo Peter Oxford/Nature Picture Library/Rex Features: p. 6; Prince of Wales Museum of Western India, Mumbai: p. 123; © Rose

Rigden, courtesy Footloose Enterprises: p. 178; photos © Roger-Viollet, courtesy Rex Features: pp. 136, 155; courtesy of Royal BC Museum Corporation: p. 20; from Sylvia Sikes, *The Natural History of the African Elephant* (Weidenfeld & Nicolson, 1971): p. 22; photo courtesy Patrick Slavenburg: p. 32; photo SNAP/Rex Features: p. 41; from Raman Sukumar, *The Living Elephants*, by permission of Oxford University Press Inc.: p. 10; from the exhibit TUSKS! of the Florida Museum of Natural History, photo by Jeff Gage © 2004: p. 14; courtesy Viv Bradshaw Foundation: p. 15; photos © Zoological Society of London: pp. 24, 44.

REPRINT PERMISSIONS

Extract from 'The Graveyard of the Elephants' published in *Kites* (Cape Town: David Philip, 1990) © Chris Mann, by permission of the author. Extract from 'The Elephant' in 'New Yoruba Poems' by E. A. Babalola published in *African Affairs* (1954) by permission of Oxford University Press. Extract from the eponymous poem in *Absence of Elephants* (Harare: College Press, 1990) © Harold Farmer, by permission of the author. Extract from 'One Elephant' published in *A Ruthless Fidelity: The Collected Poems of Douglas Livingstone*, ed. Don Maclennan and Malcolm Hacksley (Jeppestown, 2004) by permission of Monica Fairall.

Index